Microsoft® Office PowerPoint® 2016: Part 1 (Desktop/Office 365®)

Microsoft® Office PowerPoint® 2016: Part 1 (Desktop/Office 365®)

Part Number: 091060
Course Edition: 4.0

Acknowledgements

PROJECT TEAM

Author	Production Support	Media Designer	Content Editor
Bharathi G.	Tamara Hagen	Brian Sullivan	Michelle Farney

Logical Operations wishes to thank the Logical Operations Instructor Community, and in particular Joe Valentine, Suchitra S., and Nagarajan R., for their instructional and technical expertise during the creation of this course.

Notices

DISCLAIMER

TRADEMARK NOTICES

Microsoft® Office PowerPoint® 2016: Part 1 (Desktop/Office 365®)

About This Course

It's hard to imagine a day going by without people passing along large amounts of information. Messages are everywhere, and the number of messages we receive seems to be increasing each day. Whether via phone, email, mass media, or personal interaction, we are subjected to a constant stream of information. With so much communication to contend with, it can be difficult to grab people's attention. But, we are often called upon to do just that. So, how do you grab and maintain an audience's focus when you're asked to present important information? By being clear, organized, and engaging. And, that is exactly what Microsoft® Office PowerPoint® 2016 can help you do.

Gone are the days of flip charts or drawing on a white board to illustrate your point. Today's audiences are tech savvy, accustomed to high-impact multimedia content, and stretched for time. By learning how to use the vast array of features and functionality contained within PowerPoint 2016, you will gain the ability to organize your content, enhance it with high-impact visuals, and deliver it with a punch. In this course, you will use PowerPoint 2016 to begin creating engaging, dynamic multimedia presentations.

You can also use the course to prepare for the Microsoft Office Specialist (MOS) Certification exam for Microsoft PowerPoint 2016.

Course Description

Target Student

This course is designed for students who wish to gain a foundational understanding of Microsoft PowerPoint 2016 that is necessary to create and develop engaging multimedia presentations.

Course Prerequisites

To ensure success, students should be familiar with using personal computers, and should have experience using a keyboard and mouse. Students should be comfortable in the Windows® 10 environment and be able to use Windows 10 to manage information on their computers. Specific tasks the students should be able to perform include: launching and closing applications, navigating basic file structures, and managing files and folders. To meet this prerequisite, you can take either of the following Logical Operations courses:

- *Using Microsoft® Windows® 10*
- *Microsoft® Windows® 10: Transition from Windows® 8*

Course Objectives

Upon completing this course, you will be able to create and deliver engaging multimedia presentations that convey the key points of your message through the use of text, graphics, and animations.

You will:

- Identify the basic features and functions of PowerPoint 2016.
- Develop a PowerPoint presentation.
- Perform advanced text editing operations.
- Add graphical elements to your presentation.
- Modify objects in your presentation.
- Add tables to your presentation.
- Add charts to your presentation.
- Prepare to deliver your presentation.

The CHOICE Home Screen

Logon and access information for your CHOICE environment will be provided with your class experience. The CHOICE platform is your entry point to the CHOICE learning experience, of which this course manual is only one part.

On the CHOICE Home screen, you can access the CHOICE Course screens for your specific courses. Visit the CHOICE Course screen both during and after class to make use of the world of support and instructional resources that make up the CHOICE experience.

Each CHOICE Course screen will give you access to the following resources:

- **Classroom**: A link to your training provider's classroom environment.
- **eBook**: An interactive electronic version of the printed book for your course.
- **Files**: Any course files available to download.
- **Checklists**: Step-by-step procedures and general guidelines you can use as a reference during and after class.
- **LearnTOs**: Brief animated videos that enhance and extend the classroom learning experience.
- **Assessment**: A course assessment for your self-assessment of the course content.
- Social media resources that enable you to collaborate with others in the learning community using professional communications sites such as LinkedIn or microblogging tools such as Twitter.

Depending on the nature of your course and the components chosen by your learning provider, the CHOICE Course screen may also include access to elements such as:

- LogicalLABS, a virtual technical environment for your course.
- Various partner resources related to the courseware.
- Related certifications or credentials.
- A link to your training provider's website.
- Notices from the CHOICE administrator.
- Newsletters and other communications from your learning provider.
- Mentoring services.

Visit your CHOICE Home screen often to connect, communicate, and extend your learning experience!

How to Use This Book

As You Learn

This book is divided into lessons and topics, covering a subject or a set of related subjects. In most cases, lessons are arranged in order of increasing proficiency.

The results-oriented topics include relevant and supporting information you need to master the content. Each topic has various types of activities designed to enable you to solidify your understanding of the informational material presented in the course. Information is provided for reference and reflection to facilitate understanding and practice.

Data files for various activities as well as other supporting files for the course are available by download from the CHOICE Course screen. In addition to sample data for the course exercises, the course files may contain media components to enhance your learning and additional reference materials for use both during and after the course.

Checklists of procedures and guidelines can be used during class and as after-class references when you're back on the job and need to refresh your understanding.

At the back of the book, you will find a glossary of the definitions of the terms and concepts used throughout the course. You will also find an index to assist in locating information within the instructional components of the book. In many electronic versions of the book, you can click links on key words in the content to move to the associated glossary definition, and on page references in the index to move to that term in the content. To return to the previous location in the document after clicking a link, use the appropriate functionality in your PDF viewing software.

As You Review

Any method of instruction is only as effective as the time and effort you, the student, are willing to invest in it. In addition, some of the information that you learn in class may not be important to you immediately, but it may become important later. For this reason, we encourage you to spend some time reviewing the content of the course after your time in the classroom.

As a Reference

The organization and layout of this book make it an easy-to-use resource for future reference. Taking advantage of the glossary, index, and table of contents, you can use this book as a first source of definitions, background information, and summaries.

Course Icons

Watch throughout the material for the following visual cues.

Icon	Description
	A **Note** provides additional information, guidance, or hints about a topic or task.
	A **Caution** note makes you aware of places where you need to be particularly careful with your actions, settings, or decisions so that you can be sure to get the desired results of an activity or task.
	LearnTO notes show you where an associated LearnTO is particularly relevant to the content. Access LearnTOs from your CHOICE Course screen.
	Checklists provide job aids you can use after class as a reference to perform skills back on the job. Access checklists from your CHOICE Course screen.
	Social notes remind you to check your CHOICE Course screen for opportunities to interact with the CHOICE community using social media.

1 | Getting Started with PowerPoint

Lesson Time: 1 hour, 10 minutes

Lesson Introduction

You have the next great idea, and you want to pitch that idea to company leadership or to a potential client. Or, perhaps you've been called upon to present at an important function or an upcoming meeting. Regardless of the reason, you will need to express your thoughts clearly and deliver a presentation that will excite and engage your audience. You want to deliver a multimedia experience that your audience will remember.

Microsoft® Office PowerPoint® 2016 can help you organize and refine your message and deliver your presentation with style. But, you need to be familiar with how PowerPoint works before you can take advantage of its many features. You will need to know how to find what you're looking for, how to perform the basic tasks, and how to find the help you need if you get stuck along the way. That's what you'll do in this lesson.

Lesson Objectives

In this lesson, you will:

- Navigate the PowerPoint environment.

- View and navigate a presentation.

- Create and save a PowerPoint presentation.

- Use PowerPoint Help.

TOPIC A

Navigate the PowerPoint Environment

PowerPoint 2016 gives you the power and the flexibility to create an incredible array of presentations. The multimedia capabilities contained in PowerPoint allow you to add sizzle to your presentations with graphics, animation, audio, video, and a host of styles and themes. But with so many capabilities, the task of learning how to use all of PowerPoint's features can seem daunting. So, where do you begin?

To effectively use PowerPoint's many features, you must first be able to navigate your way around the user interface. Exploring the user interface and becoming familiar with the elements of PowerPoint 2016 will start you down the path to creating engaging, professional multimedia presentations.

What Is PowerPoint?

Microsoft PowerPoint 2016 is an application that is part of the Microsoft Office 2016 suite of user productivity tools. You can use PowerPoint to create, edit, and display professional-looking graphical presentations. PowerPoint presentations contain a series of slides that are used to present graphical and textual information in a logical sequence to an audience. To increase the impact of your presentations, you can add dynamic multimedia elements that engage the audience and enhance your credibility as a presenter.

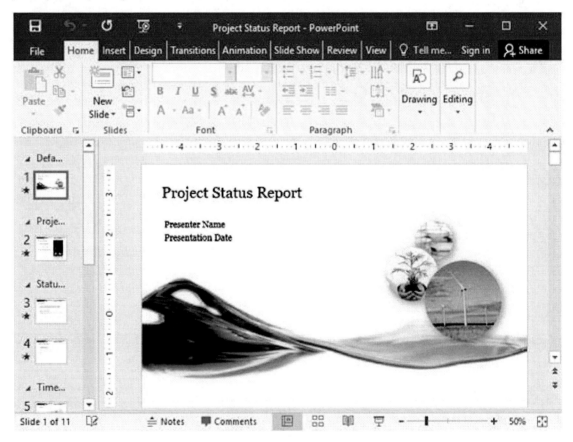

Figure 1-1: The Microsoft Office PowerPoint 2016 environment.

> **Note: PowerPoint Online App**
>
> In addition to the PowerPoint 2016 desktop application, you also have access to the PowerPoint Online app through your Office 365® subscription. Throughout this course, you will see notes that identify any significant differences between the desktop application and the online app.

Office Online Apps

When you purchase an Office 365 subscription, you also have access to the Office Online apps which include Microsoft® Excel®, Microsoft® Word, PowerPoint, Microsoft® Outlook®, and a variety of other apps. You can use any web browser to access Office 365 by navigating to **login.microsoftonline.com** and signing in with your Office 365 user account and password. These online apps are scaled-down versions of the Office 2016 desktop applications and provide basic features and some of the same functionality that exists in the desktop applications. The advantage of using the Office Online apps is the ability to access, edit, share, and store your online files across a variety of devices.

Slides

Slides are individual presentation objects that are used to display content to the audience. You can think of slides as being like individual pages of your presentation. You can use slides to display text, images, animations, charts, tables, video, and audio in your presentations.

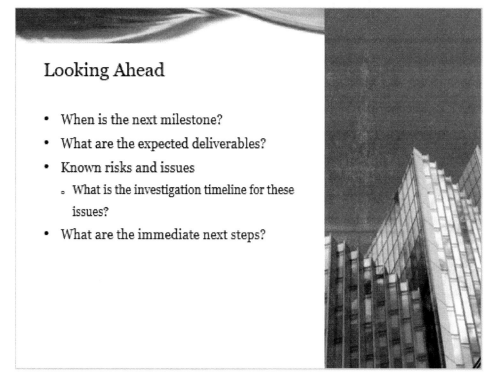

Figure 1-2: A slide in PowerPoint.

The Start Screen

When you launch PowerPoint 2016, the *Start screen* automatically displays. The **Start** screen provides you with quick access to recently used presentations and other saved PowerPoint files, templates and themes, and online resources from Microsoft. You can also choose to create a new blank presentation from the **Start** screen.

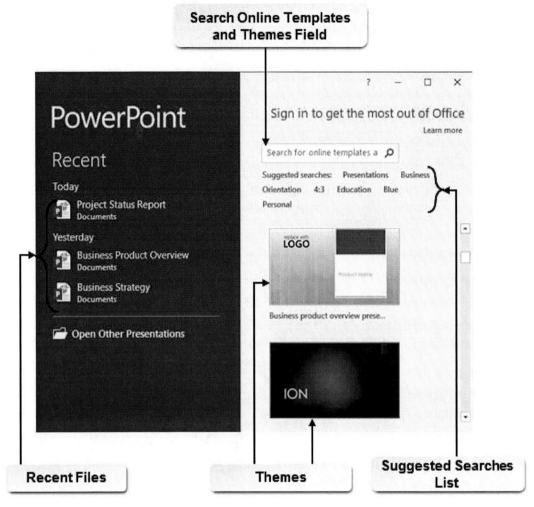

Figure 1-3: The PowerPoint 2016 Start screen.

The PowerPoint 2016 User Interface

The PowerPoint 2016 user interface contains the commands and features you will use to create and develop your presentations. Some of the key elements of the PowerPoint user interface include the title bar, **Quick Access Toolbar**, ribbon, thumbnails pane (or left pane), **Slide** pane, and status bar. These interface elements provide access to all the commands and features available in PowerPoint.

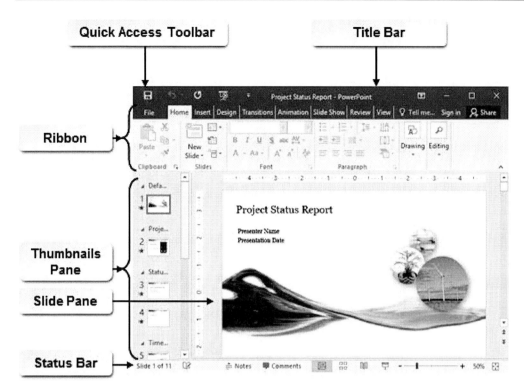

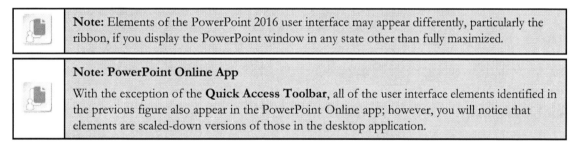

Figure 1-4: Elements of the PowerPoint 2016 user interface.

> **Note:** Elements of the PowerPoint 2016 user interface may appear differently, particularly the ribbon, if you display the PowerPoint window in any state other than fully maximized.

> **Note: PowerPoint Online App**
>
> With the exception of the **Quick Access Toolbar**, all of the user interface elements identified in the previous figure also appear in the PowerPoint Online app; however, you will notice that elements are scaled-down versions of those in the desktop application.

The Ribbon

The *ribbon* is where you will access a majority of the commands you will use to create and develop your presentation. The ribbon is a component of the PowerPoint 2016 user interface that contains task-specific command buttons and menus grouped together under a set of tabs. The ribbon provides you with a central location for accessing the various functions of PowerPoint without having to navigate the user interface extensively.

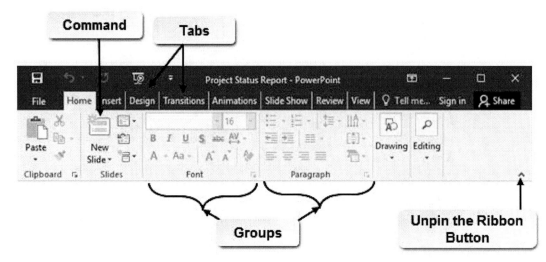

Figure 1-5: Options on the Home tab of the ribbon.

> **Note:** This course uses a streamlined notation for ribbon commands. They'll appear as "[Ribbon Tab]→[Group]→[Button or Control]" as in "select **Home**→**Clipboard**→**Paste**." Occasionally, you may already be on the tab indicated in the notation, in which case you will not need to select it.

> **Note:** Some PowerPoint 2016 command buttons are split, meaning there are actually two separate buttons you can select independently. This is often the case with commands that have multiple options/variations accessible by selecting a drop-down arrow. The **New Slide** button in the **Slides** group on the **Home** tab is an example of this. For these commands, you will be directed to either select just the button, as in "Select **Home**→**Slides**→**New Slide**," or you will be directed to select the drop-down arrow if necessary, as in "Select **Home**→**Slides**→**New Slide drop-down arrow**→**Title and Content**.

Ribbon Pinning

If you prefer to have more visual space available on your monitor, you can choose to unpin the ribbon from the user interface. This will hide the ribbon groups, leaving only the tabs displayed. When the ribbon is unpinned and you select a tab, the ribbon displays temporarily as you use a particular command or feature. You can re-pin the ribbon to the user interface at any time.

ScreenTips

When you hover the cursor over a command or a button, a *ScreenTip* may display. ScreenTips display the command name or style option, and may include a brief description of commands.

KeyTips

You might prefer to use keyboard shortcuts to perform the various tasks within PowerPoint. *KeyTips* display the corresponding keyboard shortcuts for various commands.

> **Note:** To further explore the ribbon, you can access the LearnTO **Navigate the Office 2016 Ribbon** presentation from the **LearnTO** tile on the CHOICE Course screen.

> **Note: PowerPoint Online App**
>
> It's important to remember that you are working in a browser window so while many of the common keyboard shortcuts are available, there will be instances when the keyboard shortcut behaves differently than you expect. You can find a complete list of PowerPoint Online keyboard shortcuts by opening PowerPoint Online Help and then searching for "keyboard shortcuts."

The Ribbon Tabs

Each tab in the ribbon contains a series of groups that allow you to perform related tasks. The table lists the ribbon groups and identifies the types of commands you can access in them.

Ribbon Tab	Provides You with Access To
File	Various commands, mainly related to managing files. Within the **File** tab, you can create, open, save, close, share, and print files. You can also perform other tasks, such as changing PowerPoint options and settings.
Home	The most commonly used commands for developing your presentation. Within the **Home** tab, you can add and edit text, add slides, and insert basic visual objects.
Insert	Commands for adding and working with a variety of objects, such as charts, tables, and images.
Design	Options for tailoring the overall visual design of your presentation.
Transitions	Options for creating visually appealing transitions between slides in your presentation.
Animations	Commands to add and edit animated effects in your presentation.
Slide Show	The functions you will use to deliver your final presentation.
Review	Options for reviewing and revising the content in your presentation.
View	Commands that allow you to alter how you view your presentation.

Note: PowerPoint Online App

Unlike the ribbon in the desktop app, the online app ribbon does not have the **Slide Show** and the **Review** tabs and their related commands. To use these advanced presentation and review features, you can use the **OPEN IN POWERPOINT** button in the PowerPoint Online app to open the presentation in the desktop application.

Dialog Box Launchers

Dialog box launchers are the small buttons with downward-facing arrows on the bottom-right corner of some ribbon groups. Dialog box launchers open dialog boxes or panes that contain additional commands specific to the group. These commands allow you to perform more advanced functions not directly available on the ribbon. Dialog box launchers are active only when an appropriate slide item is selected. Otherwise, they remain grayed-out.

Note: PowerPoint Online App

This feature is not available in the online app. To perform advanced commands that are not on the ribbon, you need to open the presentation in PowerPoint 2016.

The Quick Access Toolbar

The *Quick Access Toolbar* provides you with easy access to some of the most commonly used commands within PowerPoint. By default, the **Quick Access Toolbar** displays the **Save**, **Undo**, **Repeat**, and **Start from Beginning** buttons. You can customize the **Quick Access Toolbar** to include other commands that you frequently use.

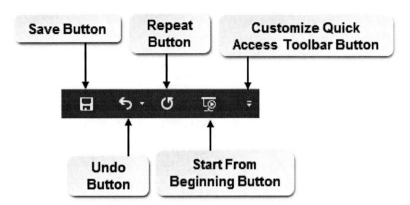

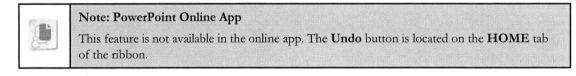

Figure 1-6: The Quick Access Toolbar with default buttons.

Note: PowerPoint Online App

This feature is not available in the online app. The **Undo** button is located on the **HOME** tab of the ribbon.

The Thumbnails Pane

By default, the *thumbnails pane* displays the slides in your presentations as a series of thumbnail images. Also referred to as the left pane, this pane provides options to navigate through the slides and access them.

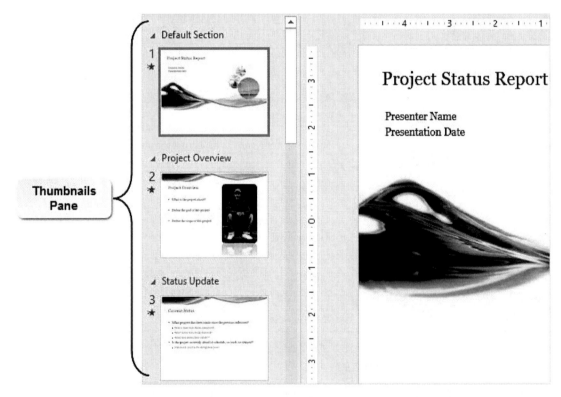

Figure 1-7: The thumbnails pane displaying thumbnail images of the slides in a presentation.

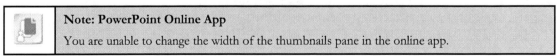

Note: PowerPoint Online App

You are unable to change the width of the thumbnails pane in the online app.

The Status Bar

The *status bar* is located across the bottom of the PowerPoint user interface. It displays information about the currently selected slide and provides you with quick access to some commonly used features.

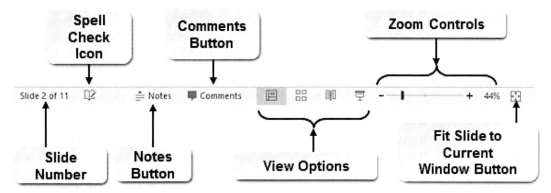

Figure 1-8: The elements in the status bar.

The following table describes the elements of the status bar.

Status Bar Element	Description
Slide number	Displays the currently selected slide number and the total number of slides in your presentation.
Spell Check icon	Displays if there are spelling errors in your presentation. You can select the icon to resolve the spelling errors.
Notes button	Displays the **Notes** pane.
Comments button	Displays the **Comments** pane.
View options	Allow you to select from among the following view options: **Normal**, **Slide Sorter**, **Reading**, and **Slide Show**.
Zoom controls	Allow you to select your desired zoom level and display the zoom percentage.
Fit slide to current window button	Displays the slide at the ideal zoom level for the current PowerPoint window.

Contextual Tabs

Contextual tabs are highly specialized tabs that appear on the ribbon when certain objects are selected. Contextual tabs contain specific commands and menus related to items such as tables, charts, and pictures. You can edit the particular attributes of these items within their respective contextual tabs. Some contextual tabs contain multiple tabs for accessing commands.

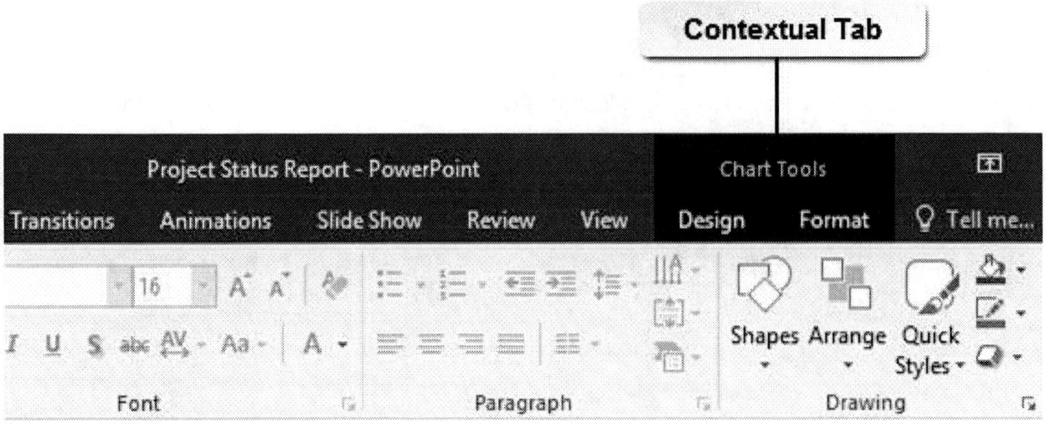

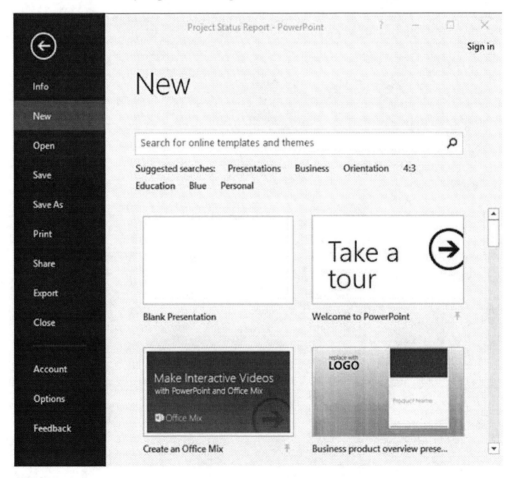

Figure 1-9: The Chart Tools contextual tab that contains multiple tabs.

The Backstage View

The *Backstage view* appears on the PowerPoint user interface when you select the **File** tab. The **Backstage** view contains vertically aligned tabs that give you access to groups of related commands and options. These commands and options allow you to perform many of the tasks associated with managing files and configuring application settings.

You can think of the **Backstage** view as where you go to do things to files. Whereas, the other ribbon tabs are where you go to do things within files.

Figure 1-10: The Backstage view with commands and options for the New tab.

> **Note: PowerPoint Online App**
>
> The structure of the **Backstage** view in PowerPoint Online is the same as described here; however, the significant difference is the absence of the **Save** and **Close** commands. When you work in any of the Office Online apps, your files are stored in your OneDrive® account and automatically updated and saved whenever you make a change. When you close the browser window, the file is closed. OneDrive is discussed more throughout the course.
>
> Another noticeable difference is the absence of the **Account** and **Options** commands in the online app. You must open PowerPoint 2016 to alter the appearance and behavior of the application.

The Open Screen

The *Open screen* is where you select the presentation you wish to open and work on. PowerPoint 2016 allows you to open files that are saved locally on your computer or a connected storage device, or online. The **Open** screen is divided into two panes which allow you to navigate to the desired location and access your files.

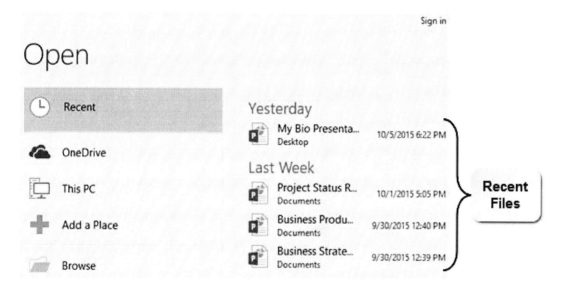

Figure 1-11: The Open screen with the list of recent files displayed.

The **Open** screen also provides options to open files from your OneDrive Personal account, Office 365® SharePoint® location, and OneDrive Business account.

> **Note:** You can open files stored in your OneDrive account only if you sign in to the corresponding Microsoft account.

> **Note: PowerPoint Online App**
>
> When you start PowerPoint Online, it opens to a special **Backstage** view landing page ready for you to open a recent document, open one stored in OneDrive, or create a new presentation.

> **Access the Checklist tile on your CHOICE Course screen for reference information and job aids on How to Access the PowerPoint 2016 Environment.**

ACTIVITY 1–1
Navigating the PowerPoint 2016 User Interface

Data File

C:\091060Data\Getting Started with PowerPoint\Develetech Ind.pptx

Scenario

You are the newest product design engineer for Develetech Industries, a manufacturer of home electronics. Develetech is known as an innovative designer and producer of high-end televisions, video game consoles, laptop and tablet computers, and mobile phones.

Develetech is a mid-sized company, employing approximately 2,000 residents of Greene City and the surrounding area. Develetech also contracts with a number of offshore organizations for manufacturing and supply-chain support.

You have been hired as part of the new product development team. You will play an active role in the research, design, and prototyping of new Develetech products. You have expertise in electrical engineering, as well as product and visual design. Additionally, you have experience managing teams of undergraduate and graduate students for major university research and design projects.

As part of Develetech's new product development team, you know you will be asked to create presentations to pitch new product ideas to your team and to company management. In your previous experience, you used a number of applications for the delivery of multimedia presentations, but never PowerPoint. Develetech Industries uses PowerPoint 2016 to create all multimedia presentations, so you realize you will need to learn how to use it. You decide the best way to start is by exploring the PowerPoint user interface.

 Note: Activities may vary slightly if the software vendor has issued digital updates. Your instructor will notify you of any changes.

1. Launch PowerPoint 2016.
    a) Select the **Start** button and select **All Apps**.
    b) In the list of apps, scroll down to the **P** section.
    c) Right-click **PowerPoint 2016**, and then select **Pin to taskbar**.
    d) On the task bar, select the **PowerPoint 2016** icon.

2. Open a presentation.
    a) In the PowerPoint 2016 **Start** screen, in the **Recent** section, select **Open Other Presentations**.
    b) Select **Browse**.
    c) Navigate to the **C:\091060Data\Getting Started with PowerPoint** folder.
    d) Select the **Develetech Ind.pptx** file and then select **Open**.

3. Explore the interface.
    a) Explore the PowerPoint 2016 environment by identifying the following elements: the **Slide** pane, the left pane, the **Quick Access Toolbar**, the ribbon, the tabs, the title bar, and the status bar.
    b) Select different ribbon tabs to explore them.

4. Unpin and re-pin the ribbon.

a) At the bottom-right corner of the ribbon, select the **Collapse the ribbon** button.

> 🔍 Find
> ab/ac Replace ▾
> ⬚ Select ▾
> Editing 　　🔼

b) Select any ribbon tab, and then select the **Pin the ribbon** button.

> 🔍 Find
> ab/ac Replace ▾
> ⬚ Select ▾
> Editing 　　📌

5. Access a contextual tab.

a) In the left pane, select **Slide 14**.
b) In the **Slide** pane, select the table.
c) On the **Table Tools** contextual tab, select the **Design** tab.
d) In the **Table Styles** group, select the **More** button.

| Transitions | Animations | Slide Show | Review | View | Design | Layout |

Table Styles

e) From the gallery that appears, select a style.

6. Access a dialog box.

a) Select the **Home** tab.
b) In the **Font** group, select the dialog box launcher.

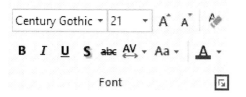

c) In the **Font** dialog box, in the **Size** text box, replace the existing value with **14**.
d) Select **OK**.

7. Explore the **Backstage** view.

a) Select the **File** tab.
b) In the **Backstage** view, select the **New** tab, and view the options displayed in the right pane.
c) Select the **Print** tab and view the options displayed in the right pane.
d) Select the back arrow button. ◀

8. Explore the **Quick Access Toolbar**.

    a) Point the cursor at the **Save** button 🖫 to view its tool tip.

    b) Select the **Customize Quick Access Toolbar** button ▾ to open the **Customize Quick Access Toolbar** menu.

▾
Customize Quick Access Toolbar
New
Open
✓ Save
Email
Quick Print
Print Preview and Print
Spelling
✓ Undo
✓ Redo
✓ Start From Beginning
✓ Touch/Mouse Mode
More Commands...
Show Below the Ribbon

    c) Check and uncheck the various options to add or remove them from the **Quick Access Toolbar**.

    d) Select **More Commands** to display the **PowerPoint Options** dialog box.

    e) From the list of commands on the left, select **Save As**, and then select **Add**.

    f) Select **OK**.

9. Save the file.

    a) On the **Quick Access Toolbar**, select the **Save As** button.

    b) In the **Save As** dialog box, navigate to the **C:\091060Data\Getting Started with PowerPoint** folder.

    c) In the **File name** text box, replace the existing text with *My Develetech Ind*

    d) Select **Save**.

TOPIC B

View and Navigate a Presentation

Now that you have explored the user interface and are becoming familiar with the elements of PowerPoint, you can start viewing presentations. It is not always easy to view presentations in the default PowerPoint view because PowerPoint presentations can contain dozens of slides.

PowerPoint 2016 offers you a variety of options for viewing and navigating your presentations. The viewing options present your content in a variety of formats and enable you to focus on different elements of your presentations. Additionally, PowerPoint 2016 provides you with options for viewing your presentation in full color, black and white, or in grayscale.

Presentation Views

There are five main viewing options in PowerPoint 2016: **Normal**, **Outline View**, **Slide Sorter**, **Notes Page**, and **Reading View**.

Presentation View	Description
Normal	Displays all of the slides in a presentation as thumbnails in the left pane. The selected slide appears in the slide pane, and the **Notes** pane displays below the slide pane. This is similar to the default view in PowerPoint.
Outline View	Displays all of the slides in a presentation as a text outline in the thumbnails pane. The outline appears only the on-slide text, and the slides do not display as thumbnail images in the left pane. The currently selected slide still displays in the slide pane as it does in the **Normal** view. This view is ideal for organizing your content or creating a storyboard.
Slide Sorter	Displays all of the slides in a presentation as large thumbnails. This view is ideal for rearranging slides.
Notes Page	Displays slides and the contents of the speaker notes in page format. This view is ideal for reviewing and editing speaker notes.
Reading View	Displays the slides on screen, one at a time. This view is similar to the final presentation your file will show to the audience.

> **Note:** There are also buttons for the **Normal**, **Slide Sorter**, and **Reading** views available on the status bar. The **Normal** button allows you to toggle between the **Normal** and the **Outline** views.

> **Note: PowerPoint Online App**
>
> In the online app, there are only three views: **Editing**, **Reading**, and **Slide Show**. The other views found in the desktop application, including the master views, are not available in the online app.

Master Views

There are three additional views: the **Slide Master** view, the **Handout Master** view, and the **Notes Master** view. The master views are the main slides that store formatting information about the entire presentation. Working within master views allows you to make universal changes to every slide, handout, or notes page associated with a presentation.

Note: To further explore slide masters, you can access the LearnTO **Use PowerPoint Slide Masters** presentation from the **LearnTO** tile on the CHOICE Course screen.

Color View Options

PowerPoint 2016 also provides you with options for viewing your presentations in various color modes. There are three color options: **Color**, **Grayscale**, and **Black and White**. In the **Black and White** or **Grayscale** mode, PowerPoint displays an additional contextual ribbon tab that provides you with further options for modifying the display colors of objects on your slides.

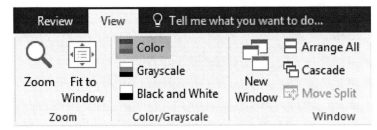

Figure 1-12: The color view options on the ribbon.

Note: PowerPoint Online App

This feature is not available in the online app. If you want to change the display colors, you must open PowerPoint 2016.

Slide Shows

A *slide show* displays your slides on screen in a particular sequence. Slide shows are how you present your slides to the audience. Slide shows display one slide at a time, allowing the audience to follow the key points of a presentation and review textual information, graphics, charts, tables, animations, and videos. PowerPoint 2016 provides you with a variety of options for presenting your slides via slide shows.

Slide Show Options

PowerPoint 2016 provides you with a variety of options for viewing and controlling your slide shows.

Slide Show Action	Mouse Action	Keyboard Shortcut
Start slide show from the beginning	Select **Slide Show→Start Slide Show→From Beginning**.	Press **F5**.
Start slide show from the current slide	Select **Slide Show→Start Slide Show→From Current Slide**, or select the **Slide Show** button on the status bar.	Press **Shift+F5**.
Go to a specific slide	N/A	Press **<slide number>+Enter**.
Advance to the next slide	Click the screen. Alternately, you can right-click the screen, and then select **Next** in the pop-up menu.	Press any one of the following keys: **N**, **Enter**, **Page Down**, the **Right Arrow**, the **Down Arrow**, or the **Spacebar**.

Slide Show Action	Mouse Action	Keyboard Shortcut
Return to the previous slide	Right-click the screen, and then select **Previous** in the pop-up menu.	Press any one of the following keys: **P**, **Page Up**, the **Left Arrow**, the **Up Arrow**, or **Backspace**.
Black out/restore the slide show	N/A	Press the **B** key.
White out/restore the slide show	N/A	Press the **W** key.
End a slide show	Right-click the screen, and then select **End Show** from the pop-up menu.	Press the **Esc** key.

> **Note:** Temporarily changing the slide to a solid black or white color can be useful when engaging in longer conversations and you want to remove the distraction of the slide being displayed. This enables you to draw the audience's attention away from the slides without having to exit the slide show.

> **Note: PowerPoint Online App**
>
> Navigating in **Slide Show** view in the online app is simplified to moving forward and backward through the slides using the techniques listed in the previous table. Additionally, you can right-click and select **Go to Slide** to quickly navigate to a slide by number. Finally, to end the show, you can press **Esc** or right-click and select **End Show**.

The Protected View

In PowerPoint 2016, all presentation files from a potentially unsafe source, such as an email attachment or the Internet, open in the **Protected View** by default. In the **Protected View**, the editing options for the presentation are disabled. When the presentation opens, the **Trust** bar will display a warning message below the tabs indicating you're viewing the file in the **Protected View**.

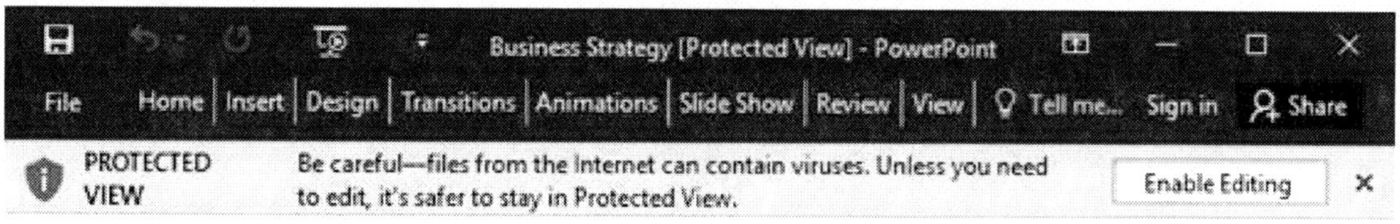

Figure 1–13: The Trust bar indicating that the presentation is open in the Protected view.

> **Note: PowerPoint Online App**
>
> This feature is not available in the online app. You must use the desktop application to open password-protected presentation files.

> Access the Checklist tile on your **CHOICE Course** screen for reference information and job aids on **How to View and Navigate a Presentation**.

ACTIVITY 1–2
Viewing and Navigating a Presentation

Before You Begin
The file My Develetech Ind.pptx is open.

Scenario
You have opened a presentation that contains many slides. Some of the slides include speaker notes. You want to make use of the viewing options in PowerPoint to take a look at the different elements in the slides. You also want to see how a complete presentation looks when it is displayed to an audience.

1. View the first three slides in the **Normal** view.
   a) In the left pane, navigate to slide **1**.
   b) Select **View→Presentation Views→Normal**.

    Note: While the presentation will launch in the **Normal** view, the **Notes** pane does not display by default. When you select the **Normal** button, the **Notes** pane displays.

   c) In the left pane, select slide **2** to review it in the **Slide** pane.
   d) In the left pane, select slide **3** to view it in the **Slide** pane.

2. View the presentation in the **Slide Sorter** view.
   a) Select **View→Presentation Views→Slide Sorter**.
   b) In the **Slide Sorter** view, use the scroll bar to view the slides.
   c) Scroll up and double-click slide **2**.

3. View a slide in the **Notes Page** view.
   a) Select **View→Presentation Views→Notes Page**.
   b) In the **Notes Page** view, review the text from the **Notes** pane.

4. View a slide show of the presentation.
   a) Select **Slide Show→Start Slide Show→From Beginning**.

    **Note:** You can also view a slide show by selecting the **Slide Show** button on the status bar.

   b) In the slide show, click the screen, or use keyboard shortcuts to advance through the slides.
   c) Type *14* and then press **Enter**.
   d) Press the **B** key to black out the presentation, and then press the **B** key again to restore the presentation.
   e) Press the **Esc** key to exit the slide show.

   Note: Alternatively, you can right-click the screen and select **End Show**.

   f) Select **File→Close** to close the file.

TOPIC C

Create and Save a PowerPoint Presentation

You are now familiar with the various elements of the PowerPoint 2016 user interface, and you are ready to create your first PowerPoint presentation. As you become more familiar with the basic functionality of PowerPoint, you will develop the confidence and the abilities you will need to create high-caliber, high-impact presentations.

To work within PowerPoint 2016, you will need to be able to create a new presentation, add various types of content, and then save and close your file.

The Default PowerPoint Presentation

When you launch PowerPoint 2016, the **Start** screen displays a selection of presentation themes and an option to create a blank presentation. A blank presentation is a presentation with no design elements and only one slide. This first slide is formatted as a title slide, with text placeholders for a title and a subtitle.

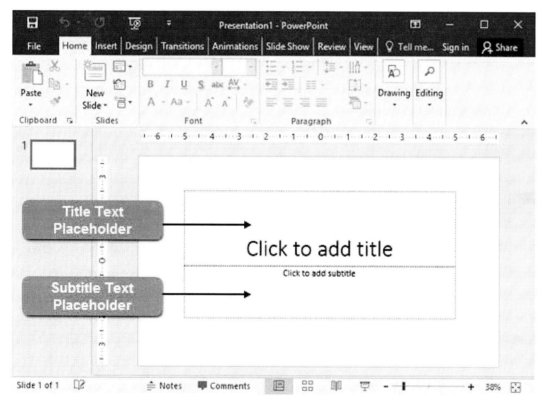

Figure 1-14: The default PowerPoint 2016 presentation.

Text Placeholders

Text placeholders, such as the title and subtitle placeholders in the default first slide, are containers for text. Text placeholders contain instructional text that indicates the type of content that you should enter in them. Text placeholders can be added or removed, resized, moved around the slide, and formatted in various ways. Slides can contain multiple text placeholders.

Notes

As you develop your presentation, you may want to add notes that you can reference when you deliver the presentation before an audience. The *Notes pane* allows you to add these speaker notes for each slide in your presentation. By default, the **Notes** pane is collapsed and is not readily visible; however, you can expand it to add notes.

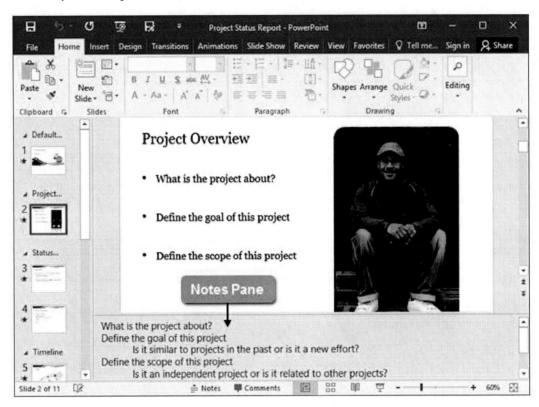

Figure 1-15: Speaker notes in the Notes pane of a slide.

> **Note: PowerPoint Online App**
> You can select the **Notes** button in the status bar to display the **Notes** pane as shown in Figure 1-15.

The Save Command

As you make progress developing your presentation, you will need to save your work. The Save command allows you to save your newly created presentation or to save the changes you make to existing presentations. Once you save a presentation, you can continue working on it or you can close the file. The default file format for PowerPoint 2016 presentations is the PPTX file format.

There are slight differences between saving a new presentation and saving an existing presentation. The first time you save a presentation, the **Save As** screen will display, allowing you to specify a file name and location. When you save an existing file, the file saves to the same location, overwriting the original file.

The Save As Command

The Save As command allows you to save a copy of an existing file to an alternate location, save a file with a different file name, or save a file in a different format.

The Save As Screen

The *Save As screen* provides you with access to the commands you will use to name and save your PowerPoint presentations. PowerPoint 2016 allows you to save your files both locally on your computer or a connected storage device, or online. Just like the **Open** screen, the **Save As** screen is also divided into two panes, which allow you to navigate to and save your presentations in the desired location. The list of recent locations will change as you work in PowerPoint further.

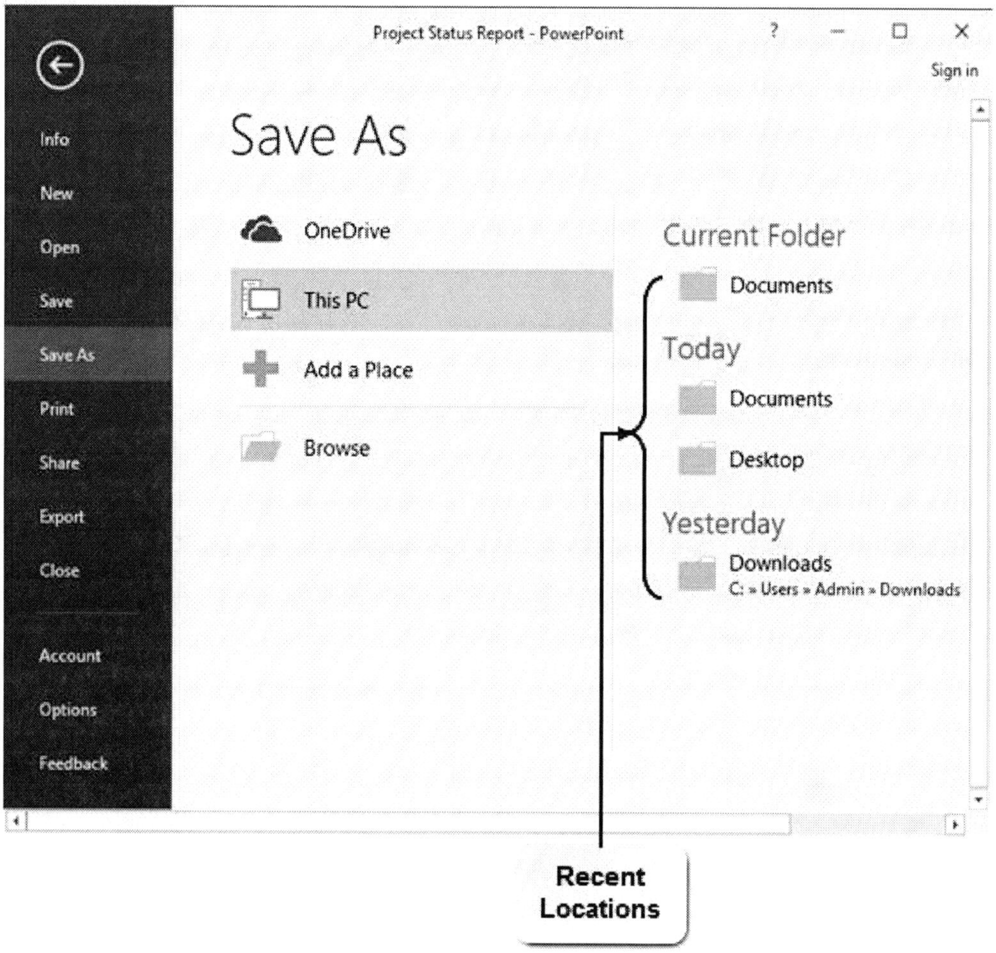

Figure 1–16: The Save As screen in PowerPoint 2016.

The **Save As** screen includes several elements that allow you to choose a location for saving your presentation.

Save As Screen Element	Used To
OneDrive	Store a presentation in the cloud using a OneDrive account associated with your Microsoft Account. OneDrive is a cloud-based service that allows you to store documents online. **Note:** To save files to OneDrive, you need to sign in to your Microsoft Account. OneDrive accounts are covered in the next section and also in greater detail in the *Microsoft® Office PowerPoint® 2016: Part 2* course.

Save As Screen Element	Used To
This PC	Save a presentation to a location in your computer. When you select this option, the most recently accessed locations on your computer are displayed in the right pane. You can select the desired location for your presentation from this list and save the file.
Add a Place	Add a location in the cloud where you need to save your presentation. Using this option, you can add an Office 365 SharePoint or a OneDrive account.
Browse	Navigate to the desired location on your computer and save your presentation at that location.

Note: PowerPoint Online App

As you work in PowerPoint Online, your presentation files are automatically updated and saved to OneDrive; therefore, you will not see a **Save** command in **Backstage** view. The **Save As** command is available to save the file with a different name but not in a different location. To save the file on your local computer, you can use the **Download a Copy** command. Keep in mind that this command is only creating a copy while the original presentation remains in OneDrive.

Access the Checklist tile on your CHOICE Course screen for reference information and job aids on How to Create and Save a PowerPoint Presentation.

ACTIVITY 1-3
Creating and Saving a PowerPoint Presentation

Before You Begin
The PowerPoint application is open.

Scenario
You have met some of the people on your new team, but not everyone. Your boss feels it would be a good idea for you to introduce yourself at the weekly departmental status meeting. She asks you to put together a brief personal biography so your new team can get to know you. You decide to use PowerPoint to outline your experiences and qualifications to present to the team. You start by creating a new presentation.

1. Create a new presentation.

   a) Select the **File** tab and, in the **Backstage** view, select **New**.

    Note: You can also press **Ctrl+N** to create a new file.

   b) Select **Blank Presentation**.

2. Add a title and subtitle to the slide.

   a) In the **Slide** pane, select the title text placeholder and type *My Bio*
   b) Select the subtitle text placeholder and type *An Introduction*
   c) Click outside the text placeholder to deselect it.

3. Add a slide to your presentation.

   a) Select **Home→Slides→New Slide**.
   b) Select the title text placeholder and type *About Me*

4. Add notes to the new slide.

   a) On the status bar, select **Notes**.
   b) Select the **Notes** pane and type a note to remind yourself to talk about projects that you have managed.

5. Save your presentation.

   a) Select the **File** tab.
   b) In the **Backstage** view, select **Save**.

    Note: You can also press **Ctrl+S** to save a new file.

   c) In the **Save As** screen, in the left pane, select **Browse**.
   d) Navigate to the **C:\091060Data\Getting Started with PowerPoint** folder.
   e) In the **File name** text box, replace the existing text with *My Bio Presentation*
   f) Select **Save**.

Microsoft OneDrive

Microsoft OneDrive provides online file storage, management, and sharing services that you can use to store, share, and collaborate on your PowerPoint presentation files as well as other types of files. There are two versions of OneDrive: personal and business. Anyone can create a personal OneDrive account, but your organization would provide you with the credentials for a business account. With a OneDrive for Business account, you have up to 1 terabyte (TB) of free OneDrive storage. However, if you have a personal Microsoft account (with an @outlook.com email address), the maximum free storage space is 5 GB. You can certainly purchase additional space if you want to.

Managing your files in OneDrive is very similar to managing files in File Explorer. The major difference is that you must upload the files to OneDrive, which enables you to access and work with your files from nearly any location using different devices. From within the OneDrive browser window, select **Upload→Files** or **Upload→Folder** and then navigate to the file or folder you want to upload. If you are working in PowerPoint 2016, another way to "upload" a file to OneDrive is to select **File→Save As** and then select **OneDrive** to be the **Save As** location.

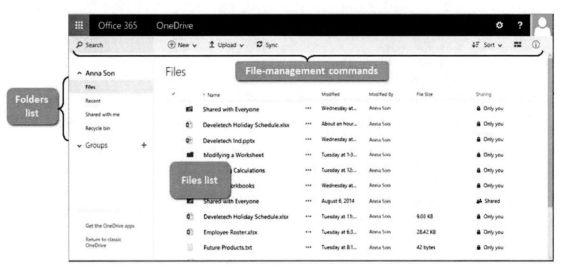

Figure 1-17: A sample OneDrive for Business page.

ACTIVITY 1-4
Signing in to Office 365 and OneDrive (Optional Instructor Demo)

Data File

C:\091060Data\Getting Started with PowerPoint\Develetech Ind.pptx

Before You Begin

You have an Office 365 login user name and password.

Scenario

Develetech now uses the Office 2016 applications through their cloud-based Office 365 subscription. While you are becoming comfortable working in the desktop versions of Office, the features of the Office 365 apps are new and unfamiliar. You're especially interested in the collaboration and mobility capabilities of these online apps. After signing in to Office 365, you'll check out the file storage app called OneDrive.

---

1. From the Windows **Start** screen, open **Microsoft Edge** and go to the Office 365 login screen and sign in to Office 365.

   a) Select the **Microsoft Edge** tile.
   b) In the **Address** box at the top of the screen, enter *https://login.microsoftonline.com*

2. Enter your credentials to sign in.

   a) In the **User ID** box, enter your user ID, including the @ symbol and the domain name.

   b) In the **Password** box, enter your password.

   c) Select **Sign in**.
   When Office 365 opens, your Outlook mail appears in the Office 365 Outlook app.

3. Open **OneDrive**.

   a) In the upper-left corner of the window, select the **App Launcher** icon.
   b) From the menu, select the **OneDrive** tile.

c) Observe the elements of the OneDrive user interface.

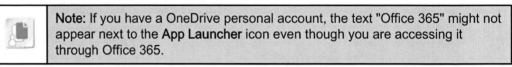

The Office 365 header at the top of the screen displays both the App Launcher and OneDrive to indicate that you are working in the online apps. At the right end of the header bar, there are buttons to access **Notifications**, **Settings**, **Help**, and your account settings, from left to right respectively. Immediately below the Office 365 header are context-specific commands. In OneDrive, these commands are used to perform basic file management tasks, such as creating new Office files as well as uploading, syncing, sorting, and viewing files.

> **Note:** If you have a OneDrive personal account, the text "Office 365" might not appear next to the **App Launcher** icon even though you are accessing it through Office 365.

4. From the student data files, upload the **Develetech Ind** file to OneDrive.
   a) From the command bar, select **Upload→Files**.
   b) In the **Open** dialog box, navigate to the **C:\091060Data\Getting Started with PowerPoint** folder.
   c) Select the **Develetech Ind.pptx** file, and then select **Open**.
   d) Observe the **Files** list.

Files

	↑ Name		Modified
	Shared with Everyone	•••	August 6, 2014
	Develetech Holiday Schedule.xlsx	•••	5 days ago
	Develetech Ind.pptx	•••	5 minutes ago

The uploaded file appears in the **Files** list.

> **Note:** You can select **Upload→Folder** to upload multiple files in an entire folder at one time. According to Microsoft, you can use the drag-and-drop method to upload files but only if you're using Microsoft® Internet Explorer® 11.

   e) Select the check mark column to the left of the file name.

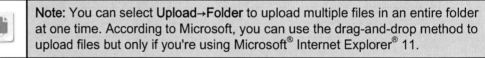

	↑ Name
	Shared with Everyone
	Develetech Holiday Schedule.xlsx
✓	Develetech Ind.pptx

f) Observe the file management commands.

| 📖 Open ∨ | 🔁 Share | 🔗 Get a link | ⬇ Download | 🗑 Delete | ➡ Move to | 📋 Copy to | ⋯ |

When a file is selected, file management commands become available. You can use these commands to delete, move, share, or otherwise manage your OneDrive files. You can access additional commands by selecting the **More commands** button. [⋯] From the **Open** command, you can open the selected file in its associated application—either the online or desktop app.

5. Open **Develetech Ind** in PowerPoint Online.
   a) From the command line, select **Open**.
   b) Select **Open in PowerPoint Online**.

PowerPoint Online opens on a separate browser tab and the presentation opens in **Reading** view.

PowerPoint Online

As part of the Office set of apps, PowerPoint Online is included in your Office 365 subscription. You can access this scaled-down version of PowerPoint through your web browser with an Internet connection. You can use PowerPoint Online to view and work with files you have saved in OneDrive, or presentation files that other users have shared with you via OneDrive.

From your Office 365 Home page, select the **App Launcher** icon ▦ and then select the **PowerPoint** tile to open PowerPoint Online. Another way to access PowerPoint Online is from within OneDrive. From the **Files** list, select a PowerPoint file and then select **Open→Open in PowerPoint Online**.

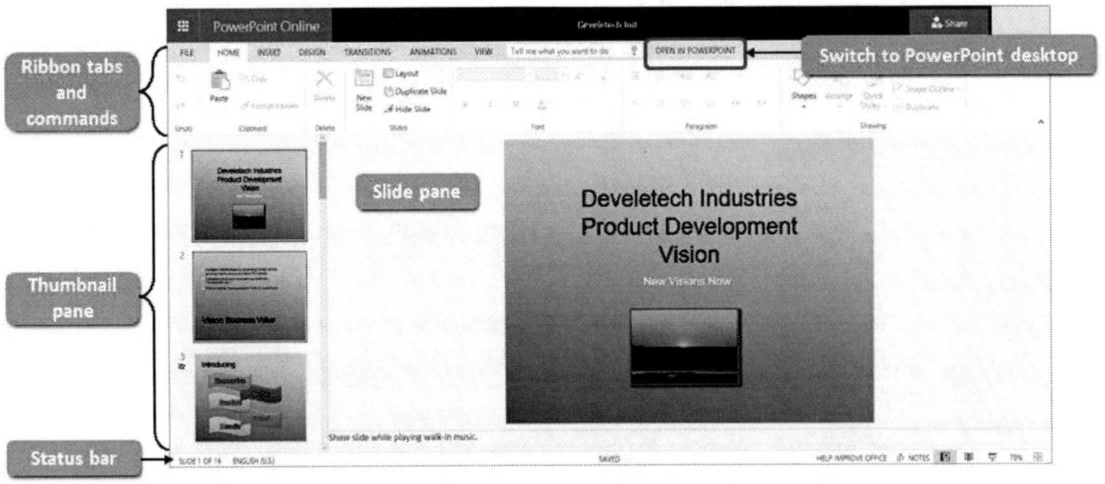

Figure 1-18: The PowerPoint user interface.

You will immediately notice that PowerPoint Online is a simplified version of the PowerPoint desktop application. There are three views in PowerPoint Online: **Reading** , **Editing** , and **Slide Show** view. Some considerations for working in PowerPoint Online are:

- By default, presentation files open in **Reading** view.
- You can select the **Start Slide Show** button to switch to **Slide Show** view. Use the following techniques to navigate through the slides.

  - To move to the next slide, use a single mouse click, select the **Next** button ⏺, or press the **Spacebar**.

  - To go back to the previous slide, select the **Back** button ⏺, or right-click and from the shortcut menu select **Previous**.

  - To end the slide show, select the **End Show** button ⏺, right-click, and from the shortcut menu, select **End Show** or press **Esc**.

- You must be in **Editing** view to make changes to the presentation file. To do so, select **Edit Presentation→Edit in PowerPoint Online**.
- In **Editing** view, you will see the familiar Office ribbon tabs and commands; however, they are scaled down from the full Office ribbon in PowerPoint 2016.
- Any changes you make to the presentation are automatically saved. There is no **Save** command in **Backstage** view.
- Use the **OPEN IN POWERPOINT** button to open the current presentation in the desktop version, provided PowerPoint 2016 is installed on the computer you are using.

ACTIVITY 1-5

Navigating in PowerPoint Online (Optional Instructor Demo)

Before You Begin

You are signed in to Office 365, and the Develetech Industries presentation file is open in PowerPoint Online.

Scenario

Before you can take full advantage of the collaboration features, you need to familiarize yourself with the PowerPoint Online user interface.

---

1. In **Reading** view, use the slide navigation commands to navigate through the presentation.

   You can use the left- and right-pointing arrows to move to the previous or next slides, respectively. To quickly go to a specific slide, select the **Slide 1 of 16** indicator to display a list of slides by title.

2. Display **Slide Show** view and navigate through the slides in the presentation.

   a) From the commands at the top of the window, select the **Start Slide Show** button.

   b) Use the **Next** button ⊙ several times to advance through the slides.

   c) Right-click an empty area of the slide to display the shortcut menu.

   > Next
   > Previous
   > Go to Slide...
   > End Show

   d) Select **End Show** to return to **Reading** view.

    Note: You can also use the keyboard keys to move to the next (**N**, **Page Down**, or **Spacebar**) and the previous (**P**, **Page Up**) slides. To end the slide show, press **Esc**.

3. Edit the presentation in PowerPoint Online.

---

a) In the command bar, select **Edit Presentation→Edit in PowerPoint Online**.

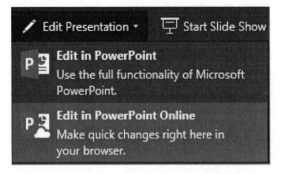

b) Observe the available ribbon tabs and commands.

While many of the tabs are the same as those on the familiar PowerPoint 2016 ribbon, there are some differences. At first glance, the **Slide Show** and **Review** tabs are not included, and the buttons that do exist appear larger and slightly simplified. Additionally, there are no dialog box launchers in the PowerPoint Online ribbon.

c) In the **Thumbnails** pane, select slide **3**.
   You can use the **Thumbnails** pane to navigate through the slides. The only significant difference is the inability to change the width of the pane.

4. **Create a new slide with the your name in the title.**

   a) Select slide **1**.
   b) On the ribbon, select **HOME→Slides→New Slide**.
   c) In the **New Slide** dialog box, verify that **Title and Content** is selected and then select **Add Slide**.
   d) Select the **Title** placeholder.

   ![CLICK TO ADD TITLE]

   e) Type *[your name]*

f) Select the **Content** placeholder.

You can easily add text by typing in the **Content** placeholder. The arrow bullet was applied in PowerPoint 2016 so it is preserved when the file is opened in PowerPoint Online. When you select the text box, the underlying (or default) bullets are displayed.

g) Select slide **1** and select the picture image.
h) Drag the top-left sizing handle to increase the image size.
You can resize and rotate slide objects just as you can in the desktop application.

5. **Observe the available tools on the PowerPoint Online ribbon tabs.**

a) On slide 1, select the two-line title text, **Develetech Industries Product Development Vision**.
b) Select **HOME→Font→Italic**.
c) Select the subtitle text **New Visions Now** and then select **HOME→Font→Increase Font Size**.
d) Select the **INSERT** tab.
You can insert tables, images, illustrations, hyperlinks, text boxes, comments, symbols and online videos.
e) Select the **DESIGN** tab and from the **Variants** group, select a color of your choice.
You can change the appearance of the presentation by applying a different theme or background color. If you want to create a theme, you will need to work in PowerPoint 2016.
f) Select the **TRANSITIONS** tab.
Any transitions that were created in the desktop application will be preserved when you view or run the slide show in the online app. There is a limited number of slide transitions that you can apply, but you must use PowerPoint 2016 to edit the transitions.
g) Select the **ANIMATIONS** tab.
Like slide transitions, you have a limited number of animations that can be applied, but if you want to edit the animations, you must open the presentation in the desktop application.

6. **Save the edited presentation file.**

a) Select **FILE** to access **Backstage** view.

b) From the commands on the left, select **Save As**.

c) Observe the text under **Where's the Save Button?**
If PowerPoint Online is new to you, this might be the biggest difference from PowerPoint 2016. As the message explains, your presentation is automatically saved.

7. Observe the remaining commands and tabs in the **Backstage** view.

a) Select **Info**.

As noted, you must open the presentation in PowerPoint 2016 to view the presentation properties and have access to the full functionality of the application.

b) In the left pane, select **New**.

You can create a new blank presentation or select from a list of available templates. However, you are unable to search for online templates like you can in PowerPoint 2016.

c) In the left pane, select **Open**.
   You are only able to choose from **Recent Documents** or select the **OneDrive** link to access more files. There's no option to open files stored anywhere else.

d) Observe the other **FILE** tab options: **Print**, **Share**, **About**, and **Help**.
   The settings found on these tabs provide the information and settings you'd expect.

e) Select the **Back** button ⊖ to return to the presentation.

8. Open the **Develetech Ind** in PowerPoint 2016.

a) In the PowerPoint Online command bar, select the **OPEN IN POWERPOINT** button.
   If the presentation opens in PowerPoint 2016 without any problems, you can close the message box in PowerPoint Online.

b) Activate the browser window and close the **PowerPoint Online** tab.

| ☁ Files - OneDrive | 🔲 Develetech Ind.pptx ✕ |

This is the equivalent of selecting **File→Close** in PowerPoint 2016.

c) Close the browser window. If prompted, close all open tabs.

d) Observe the updated presentation.

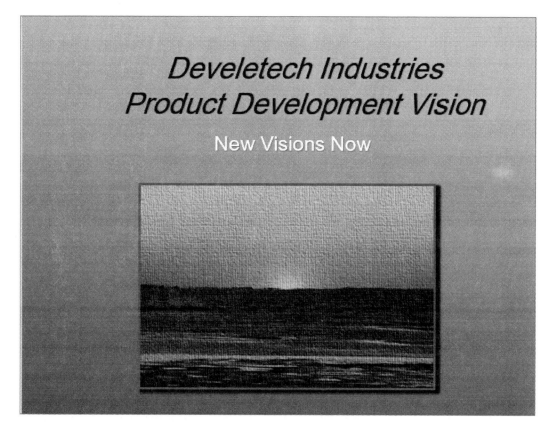

You should see the edits that were made to the presentation in PowerPoint Online.

9. Select **File→Close** to close the file without saving it.

TOPIC D

Use PowerPoint Help

As you become more proficient with PowerPoint, and you begin to use more of its advanced features, it is likely that you will come across a command, a menu, or a function with which you are unfamiliar. When that happens, you may be tempted to experiment with the item until you discover how to use it properly, which can result in delays and wasted effort.

PowerPoint contains a built-in help system to assist you in such circumstances. Understanding how PowerPoint's help features work is one of the fastest ways to find answers to your questions. It can also help you become a more proficient PowerPoint user.

PowerPoint 2016 Help

PowerPoint 2016 Help is a collection of information designed to answer your questions about the various functions and features of PowerPoint 2016. This feature enables you to specify a query and search for articles related to the tasks you perform within PowerPoint. When your search is completed, the **PowerPoint 2016 Help** window is populated with links to relevant resources that answer your query.

The **PowerPoint 2016 Help** window also displays categories of PowerPoint features and provides links to Help pages relevant to them. To access the PowerPoint 2016 Help feature, you need to be connected to the Internet. PowerPoint 2016 does not provide Help resources offline.

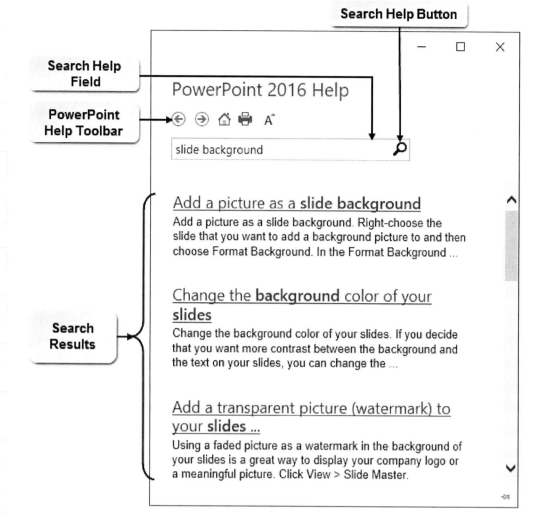

Figure 1-19: The PowerPoint 2016 Help window with links to resources.

> **Note: PowerPoint Online App**
>
> You can access the PowerPoint Online Help window by selecting **File→Help→Help**. Another option is to enter a keyword in the **Tell Me** search box and then select the **Get Help on** item in search results pane. Once open, the PowerPoint Online Help window works the same as the PowerPoint 2016 Help window.

The PowerPoint Help Interface

The PowerPoint 2016 Help interface consists of the PowerPoint Help toolbar and the **Search** field. The PowerPoint Help toolbar provides you with a quick means of navigating through the PowerPoint Help pages. The **Search** field allows you to tailor your search by filtering results relevant to a specific topic.

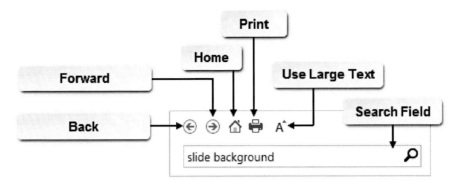

Figure 1-20: The PowerPoint 2016 Help interface with the toolbar and Search field.

The following table describes the PowerPoint 2015 Help options.

PowerPoint Help Toolbar Button	Function
Back	Navigates to the previous **Help** page.
Forward	Navigates to the next **Help** page. This button is active only once the **Back** button has been used.
Home	Returns to the **PowerPoint 2016 Help** home page.
Print	Prints the displayed **Help** page.
Use Large Text	Toggles between a magnified view and a standard view of the **PowerPoint 2016 Help** window.

The Tell Me Feature

Tell Me is a new feature in PowerPoint 2016 that enables you to quickly find specific functions within the PowerPoint interface. When you type what you're looking for in the **Tell Me** text box, PowerPoint provides a menu of matching commands beneath the text box. You can select a command to perform it immediately, or you can add it to the **Quick Access Toolbar**. In this way, **Tell Me** helps you save the time it takes to locate a command in the ribbon.

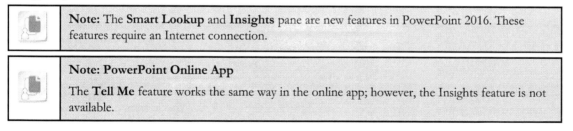

Figure 1–21: The Tell Me text box with results.

The Get Help and Smart Lookup Options

When you search for a command using the **Tell Me** feature, you can also access Help pages for the command by using the **Get Help** and **Smart Lookup** options. While the **Get Help** option displays links to Help pages in the **PowerPoint 2016 Help** window, the **Smart Lookup** option searches the Internet for information on the command and displays links to relevant resources in the new **Insights** pane.

> **Note:** The **Smart Lookup** and **Insights** pane are new features in PowerPoint 2016. These features require an Internet connection.

> **Note: PowerPoint Online App**
>
> The **Tell Me** feature works the same way in the online app; however, the Insights feature is not available.

The Insights Feature

Insights is a new feature in PowerPoint 2016 that uses the Bing® search tool to perform a smart lookup operation on the Internet. You can use the Insights feature to research the content in your presentation, as well as to access more information on PowerPoint features. When a smart lookup operation is performed, the **Insights** pane displays links to resources on the Internet that are contextually relevant to your content.

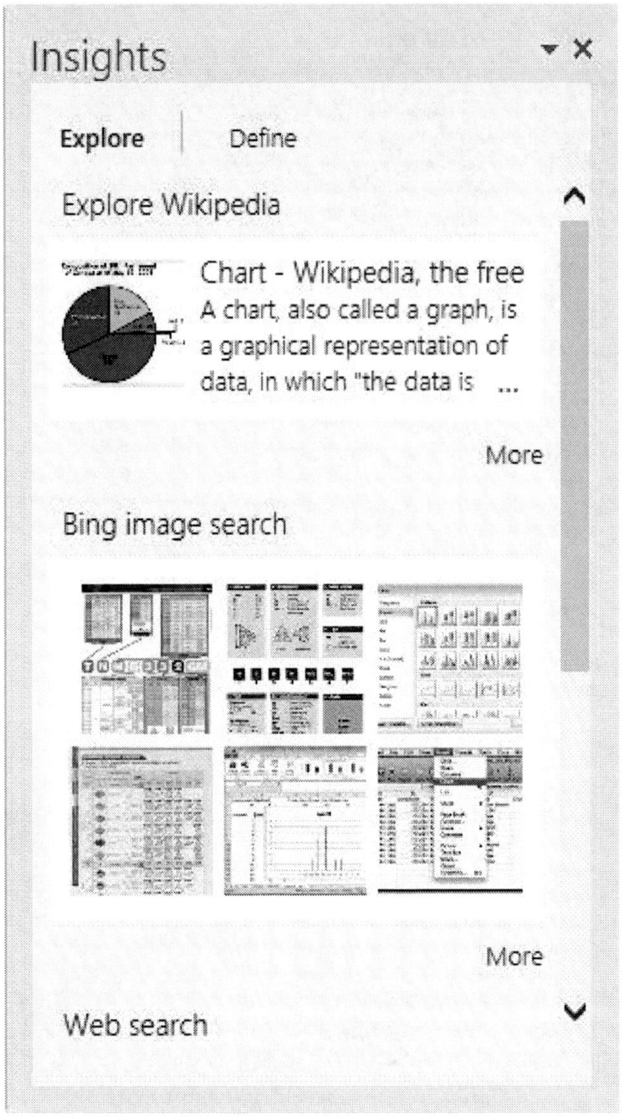

Figure 1-22: The Insights pane with search results.

Note: You will learn more about the Insights feature when you review a presentation in a later lesson.

Access the Checklist tile on your CHOICE Course screen for reference information and job aids on How to Use PowerPoint Help.

ACTIVITY 1-6
Using PowerPoint Help

Data File

C:\091060Data\Getting Started with PowerPoint\My Picture.jpg

Before You Begin

The My Bio Presentation.pptx file is open.

Scenario

You want to enhance your presentation by adding more content to it. However, you are not yet familiar with the commands and features in PowerPoint and their location on the ribbon. Instead of experimenting with the commands on your own, you would like to save time and effort by getting assistance through the PowerPoint 2016 Help and Tell Me features.

---

1. **Search PowerPoint 2016 Help for information.**

   a) On the ribbon, select the **File** tab.

   b) In the **Backstage** view, at the top-right corner, select the **Microsoft PowerPoint Help** button. ?

    Note: Alternatively, you can press the **F1** key to access PowerPoint 2016 Help.

   c) In the **PowerPoint 2016 Help** window, in the **Search** text box, type *add table*

   d) Select the **Search** button. 🔎
   e) From the list of search results, select the first link and review the information.
   f) Select the **Close** button.

2. **Access a command using the Tell Me feature.**

   a) In the **Backstage** view, at the top-left corner, select the **Back Arrow** button.
   b) In the **Slide** pane, select the content placeholder.
   c) On the ribbon, in the **Tell me what you want to do** text box, type *add image*

View	💡 add image
Hyperlink	🖼 **Image (ActiveX Control)**
	🖼 Online Pictures
	🖼 Insert Pictures
Link	🖼 Photo Album ▸
· 3 · · · I ·	Slide Image
	❓ Get Help on "add image"
	ⓘ Smart Lookup on "add image"

   d) From the drop-down list of search results, select **Insert Pictures**.
   e) Navigate to the **C:\091060Data\Getting Started with PowerPoint** folder.

---

f) Select the **My Picture.jpg** file and then select **Insert**.

g) Select **File→Save** to save the changes.

 Note: You can also save the changes by selecting the **Save** button from the **Quick Access Toolbar** or by pressing **Ctrl+S**.

h) Select **File→Close** to close the file.

Summary

In this lesson, you started using Microsoft PowerPoint 2016. You navigated the user interface, opened a presentation, created and saved your first PowerPoint presentation, and used the PowerPoint 2016 Help features. Developing these skills provides you with a foundation to build upon. With these skills in hand, you can be confident that you will be able to begin using the more complex features in PowerPoint 2016.

How might your experience using other Microsoft Office applications apply to using PowerPoint 2016? How is PowerPoint 2016 similar to the other applications you have used? How is it different?

Which tasks that you have been assigned in the past would have been easier to accomplish using PowerPoint 2016?

Note: Check your CHOICE Course screen for opportunities to interact with your classmates, peers, and the larger CHOICE online community about the topics covered in this course or other topics you are interested in. From the Course screen you can also access available resources for a more continuous learning experience.

2 Developing a PowerPoint Presentation

Lesson Time: 1 hour

Lesson Introduction

You are now familiar with the basic functions of Microsoft® Office PowerPoint® 2016, and you are ready to develop presentations that you can use in your daily working life. Although you already know how to add slides and basic text to your presentations, you will certainly wish to craft presentations with a bit more substance.

With PowerPoint, you can choose from among several presentation types, apply a variety of themes and templates, and take advantage of powerful text editing capabilities. These allow you to spend less time working on your presentation and more time focusing on your message and how to deliver it.

Lesson Objectives

In this lesson, you will:

- Select a presentation type.

- Edit text.

- Build a presentation.

TOPIC A

Select a Presentation Type

You can now begin developing presentations to deliver key messages to your audience, and you will want to craft those presentations to suit particular situations. PowerPoint offers a wide range of options for customizing and optimizing your presentations, including pre-formatted templates and the ability to create presentations from pre-existing files.

Using these features will allow you to create engaging, dynamic presentations without the time investment required to create presentations from scratch every time.

Templates

In PowerPoint, a *template* is an existing presentation containing content placeholders that are already formatted. There are thousands of templates on **Office.com** that you can use to create a presentation in PowerPoint 2016. Or, you can create new templates from existing presentations. The file format for PowerPoint templates is the POTX file.

Figure 2–1: A set of PowerPoint 2016 templates.

Note: To further explore templates, you can access the LearnTO **Decide Between PowerPoint Templates and Themes** presentation from the **LearnTO** tile on the CHOICE Course screen.

Methods to Create Presentations

There are three methods for creating a presentation within PowerPoint 2016. These methods include creating a blank presentation, searching for a template or theme in **Office.com** and using it to create a presentation, and creating a presentation based on a theme available within PowerPoint 2016. The PowerPoint **Start** screen and the **New** screen provide options to create a new presentation.

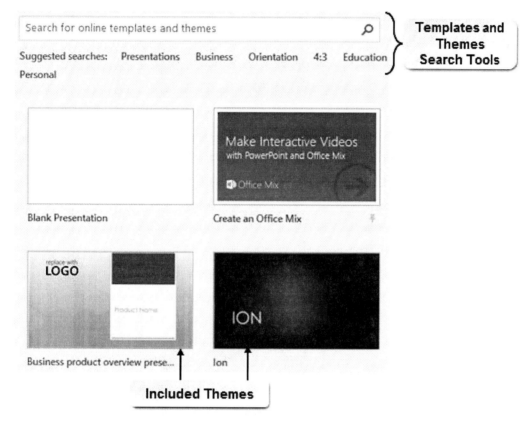

Figure 2-2: Options to create a new presentation.

The following table describes the theme options available.

Option	Description
Blank Presentation	Creates a presentation that has a single title slide with no design formatting.
Templates and Themes Search	Creates a presentation from one of the many templates or themes available from **Office.com**.
Included Themes	Creates a presentation from one of the themes included with PowerPoint 2016.

Note: Themes are covered in-depth later in this lesson.

Outlines

You can also create a PowerPoint presentation from an existing Microsoft® Word outline. The heading styles featured in Word, or any other application that supports heading styles, will create the structure for the presentation. Only the title and the heading text will import to the PowerPoint presentation. Body text from papers and reports authored in Word will not open in the presentation.

Note: PowerPoint Online App

With the exception of creating a presentation from a Word outline, you can use the same methods that are described to create new presentations. PowerPoint templates are available in **Backstage** view by selecting **FILE→New**. If the template you are searching for is not listed, you can go directly to **office.com** and select **Templates** at the top of the page. The Office templates are organized by category and when you find the template you want to use, simply select it and then select **Open in PowerPoint Online**. The downloaded template will be stored in OneDrive®.

Access the Checklist tile on your CHOICE Course screen for reference information and job aids on How to Select a Presentation Type.

ACTIVITY 2-1
Creating a Presentation from a Template

Scenario

You realize that by starting with a blank presentation, you will have to do far more work to put together your brief personal bio. You decide using one of the templates available for PowerPoint is a much better starting point for your presentation. You noticed a colleague working on a training presentation that you felt would also make a good personal bio presentation. So, you search for the template to use for your presentation.

> **Note:** Activities may vary slightly if the software vendor has issued digital updates. Your instructor will notify you of any changes.

1. Search for the required template.
   a) Select **File→New**.
   b) In the **Search for online templates and themes** text box, type *training*
   c) Select the **Start searching** button. 🔍

2. Create your presentation.
   a) In the list of search results, select the **Training presentation** template that looks like the following.

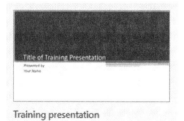

   Training presentation

   b) In the template's window, select **Create**.

3. Save your presentation.
   a) In the **Quick Access Toolbar**, select **Save**.
   b) Navigate to the **C:\091060Data\Developing a PowerPoint Presentation** folder.
   c) In the **File name** text box, replace the default text with *My Bio* and select **Save**.
   d) Close the presentation.

TOPIC B

Edit Text

Text is one of the most critical elements of any presentation. It is the basic method by which you will deliver the information your audience needs. As you develop your presentation, you are likely to encounter changes that you would like to make. And, let's face it, we all make mistakes. You will need to make some revisions to the text in your presentation.

Knowing how to enter and edit text will enable you to correct errors, focus your message, and deliver your presentation effectively. PowerPoint also gives you the ability to use existing text from other slides and documents to save precious development time.

Text Boxes

It may be necessary to insert additional containers for the text on the slides in your presentation. *Text boxes* are another type of text container you can add to your slides. Unlike text placeholders, text boxes contain no instructional text. Text boxes are blank when you add them to a slide.

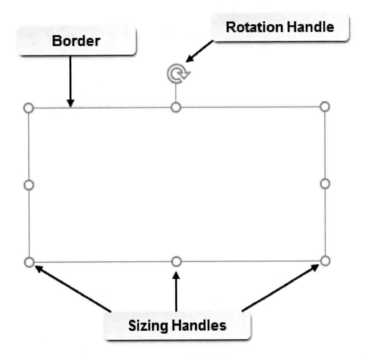

Figure 2–3: A text box with a border, a rotational handle, and sizing handles.

Like text placeholders, text boxes can be added or removed, resized, moved around the slide, and formatted in various ways. Text boxes can contain multiple lines of text. By default, typed text will wrap down to the next line when it reaches the text box border. By default, the vertical height of the text box and the text's font size will automatically adjust when the amount of text exceeds the text box's borders. However, you do have the option to lock the font size within a text box.

 Note: Most of the text you will add to your presentations, title text, subtitle text, general body text, bullet lists, and so on, will be added within text boxes. However, other objects, such as shapes, can also contain text. Adding text to other objects will be covered in later lessons.

The Sizing Handles

You can use the *sizing handles* to increase or decrease the size of on-slide objects, such as text boxes and images. The sizing handles on the corners of the text box will adjust both its vertical and horizontal borders simultaneously.

The Rotation Handle

You can use the *rotation handle* to rotate on-slide objects. Text within text boxes and text placeholders will rotate with the object.

> **Access the Checklist tile on your CHOICE Course screen for reference information and job aids on How to Add and Remove Text Boxes.**

Text Selection Methods

PowerPoint offers you several options for selecting the text you wish to edit. Selected text will appear highlighted on the screen.

Text Selection	Method
Specific section of text	• Click and drag with the mouse to select a section of text. • Place the cursor to the left of the text you wish to begin highlighting. Then, press and hold the **Shift** key and select to the right of the last character of text you wish to highlight. • Place the cursor next to the text you wish to begin highlighting. Then, press and hold down the **Shift** key and use the arrow keys to extend the highlighted portion of text in any direction.
A single word	Double-click the word. This will also highlight the space following the selected word, but it will not highlight punctuation.
A paragraph or a bulleted item	Triple-click the text.
Non-contiguous sections of text (sections of text that are not adjacent)	Use any of the text selection methods to highlight the first section of text you wish to select. Then, press and hold the **Ctrl** key, and then select the next desired section of text.
All text within a selected text placeholder	• Press **Ctrl+A**. • Select **Home→Editing→Select**, and then, from the drop-down menu, select **Select All**.

> **Note: PowerPoint Online App**
>
> You can use the single-click and double-click methods to quickly select text; however, the triple-click is not available in the online app. Additionally, you are not able to select non-contiguous text at the same time.

The Mini Toolbar

The *Mini toolbar* is a floating toolbar that appears next to highlighted text. The **Mini** toolbar allows you to access some of the most commonly used text edit options without having to navigate to them on the ribbon. The **Mini** toolbar will disappear as you move the cursor away from it or the selected text.

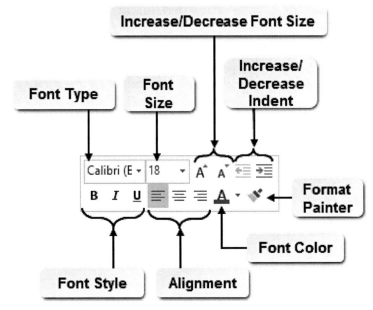

Figure 2-4: The Mini toolbar with text formatting options.

> **Note:** The **Mini** toolbar will also appear when you right-click within certain objects, such as tables. It also appears with different commands for objects such as pictures and charts.

The Cut, Copy, and Paste Options

PowerPoint offers you a variety of methods for moving selected text around on slides, from one slide to another, or from other sources into your presentation. You can use the **Cut**, **Copy**, and **Paste** options to move text within your presentation.

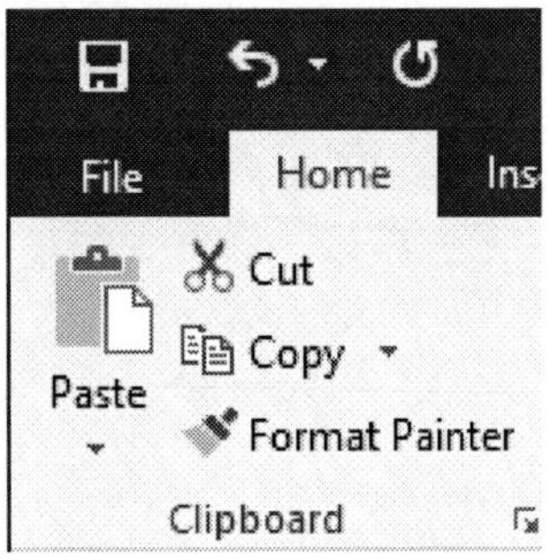

Figure 2-5: The Cut, Copy, and Paste options.

The **Cut** option will remove the selected text, whereas the **Copy** option will copy the text but leave the original text in place. Both of these options place a temporary copy of the text on the clipboard. You can then place a copy of the text in a new location in any text placeholder within your presentation.

> **Note:** The Cut, Copy, and Paste functions are the same for slides and for objects other than text, including text boxes.

Alternate Methods to Cut, Copy, and Paste

There are also keyboard shortcuts that allow you to perform the Cut, Copy, and Paste functions.

Function	Keyboard Shortcut
Cut	**Ctrl+X**
Copy	**Ctrl+C**
Paste	**Ctrl+V**

> **Note: PowerPoint Online App**
>
> The Cut, Copy, and Paste commands function the same in the online app; however, the first time you use the **Paste** command, you are prompted to allow the web page to access the clipboard. Additionally, the **Paste** command is a simple, straightforward paste. None of the advanced paste options are available. To use the paste options, you must open the presentation in PowerPoint 2016.

The Clipboard

Anything you cut or copy in Office 2016 applications is stored on a task pane called the *clipboard*. All items on the clipboard, whether from your presentation, other PowerPoint presentations, or other Office applications, are available for pasting into your presentation.

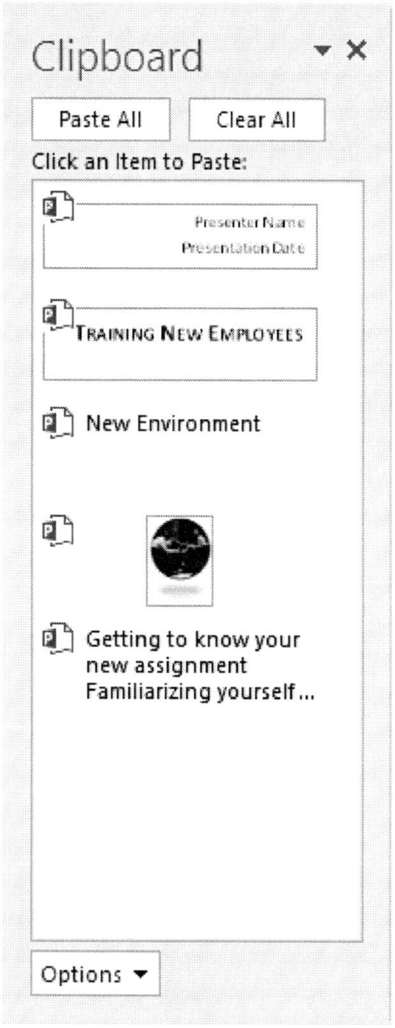

Figure 2-6: Contents stored in the clipboard.

Selecting an item on the clipboard will paste that item to the insert point in your presentation. The **Paste All** option will paste all of the items on the clipboard to the insert point, and the **Clear All** button will delete all items from the clipboard.

> **Note: PowerPoint Online App**
>
> While the cut, copy, and paste actions use the clipboard, you are not able to display the **Clipboard** pane and have access to the various paste options. To perform advanced paste actions, you need to open the presentation in PowerPoint 2016.

The Clipboard Paste Options

It is likely that not all of the text within your presentation will have the same formatting. Likewise, text copied to the clipboard from other applications may have different formatting than the text in your presentation. The clipboard offers you several paste options to accommodate these textual differences.

Paste Option	Effect
Use Destination Theme	The pasted text will adopt the formatting of the theme applied to the destination text box.
Keep Source Formatting	The pasted text retains its original formatting.
Picture	The text will be pasted as an image. When you use this paste option, you cannot edit the pasted text.
Keep Text Only	Only unformatted text is pasted.

The Paste Preview Option

Paste Preview is a temporary preview of the result of a paste command. The paste preview is displayed at the insertion point on a slide when you hover the mouse pointer over a paste option in the **Paste** drop-down menu. As you hover over the different options, the preview displays how the pasted text would appear when a particular option is selected.

The Paste Special Command

The *Paste Special command* allows you to paste items to a new location as a specific type of file. For example, you can paste a JPG file to your presentation as a PNG file. The **Paste Special** dialog box provides you with the paste options for the selected item.

Paste Special			? ✕

Source: Unknown Source

As:

○ Paste
○ Paste link

HTML Format	^
Formatted Text (RTF)	
Unformatted Text	
Picture (PNG)	
Picture (Enhanced Metafile)	
Picture (JPEG)	∨

☐ Display as icon

Result

Pastes the contents of the Clipboard into your presentation as HTML Format.

OK   Cancel

Figure 2-7: The Paste Special dialog box.

> **Note: PowerPoint Online App**
>
> This feature is not available in the online app. To use the **Paste Special** command, you must open the presentation in PowerPoint 2016.

Galleries

Galleries are rectangular menus that display a variety of related visual options. These options appear as thumbnail images and provide you with sets of predefined styles for art, pictures, and text that you can apply to your presentation.

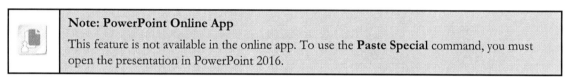

Artistic Effects Options...

Figure 2-8: The Artistic Effects gallery.

The Live Preview Feature

The *Live Preview feature* displays a view of formatting changes to your presentation without actually applying the changes. These previews appear when you hover the mouse pointer over the various options in some galleries. This feature can save you time when you need to create a highly stylized presentation.

 Access the Checklist tile on your CHOICE Course screen for reference information and job aids on How to Edit Text.

ACTIVITY 2-2
Editing Text

Data Files

C:\091060Data\Developing a PowerPoint Presentation\Bio Presentation.pptx

C:\091060Data\Developing a PowerPoint Presentation\Dexter_Collingsworth_Resume.docx

Before You Begin

Microsoft Word 2016 is installed.

Scenario

The training template is a good starting point for your presentation, but you will need to make changes. You decide to revise some of the text and include information from your resume.

---

1. Navigate to the **C:\091060Data\Developing a PowerPoint Presentation** folder and open the **Bio Presentation** file.

2. Change the title text on the title slide.
   a) If necessary, in the left pane, navigate to slide **1**.
   b) In the title text box, select the **Title of Training Presentation** text.
   c) Replace the text by typing *My Bio*
   d) Click outside the title text box to deselect it.

3. Replace the subtitle text.
   a) In the subtitle text box, select the **Presented by Your Name** text.
   b) Type *An Introduction*
   c) Click outside the text box to deselect it.

4. Launch a Word document.
   a) Open File Explorer.
   b) Navigate to the **C:\091060Data\Developing a PowerPoint Presentation** folder.
   c) Double-click the **Dexter_Collingsworth_Resume.docx** file.

5. Copy text from the resume document.
   a) In the Word document, in the **Technical Skills** section, select the entire bulleted list.
   b) Select **Home→Clipboard→Copy**.

    Note: Alternatively, you can use **Ctrl+C** to copy the text.

6. Paste the copied text into a slide.
   a) Switch to the **Bio Presentation.pptx** file in the PowerPoint window.
   b) Navigate to slide **2**.
   c) Select all of the bulleted list text.
   d) Select the **Home→Clipboard→Paste** down arrow, and then select **Use Destination Theme**.

Note: In some instances, you can also use the **Ctrl+V** keys for pasting text. However the key command does not allow you to use the different **Paste** options, such as **Use Destination Theme**.

e) Replace the existing title text on the slide with *My Skills*

7. Rearrange the text on the slide.

a) Triple-click the second bullet point to select all of the text in the bullet point.

b) While holding the **Ctrl** key, click and drag the text by moving the cursor immediately before the word "Working" in the first bullet point.

c) Ensure that a copy of the selected text is placed at the top of the bulleted list, and then release the **Ctrl** key.

Note: At this point, there are two bulleted list items with the same text. These steps demonstrate how to create a copy of the selected bulleted item for instructional purposes. You will be removing the original item in the next step.

d) Select the original version of the text (now the third bullet) by triple-clicking the text, and then press the **Delete** key.

e) Click outside the text box to deselect it.

8. Edit text in another slide.

a) In the left pane, navigate to slide **7** titled "Lesson 2: Objectives."

b) Select the title text, and replace it by typing *Today's Overview*

c) Select all of the text in the first bullet point and type *My Qualifications*

d) Similarly, replace the existing text in the second bullet point with *My Experience*

e) Replace the existing text in the third bullet point with *Questions*

9. Save the changes to the file.

a) Select **File→Save As**.

b) Navigate to the **C:\091060Data\Developing a PowerPoint Presentation** folder.

c) In the **File name** text box, replace the default text with *My Bio Presentation* and select **Save**.

TOPIC C

Build a Presentation

As you develop your presentation, it will naturally increase in size and complexity. You will likely need to add additional information, use slides of varying styles, rearrange your slides, and decide on a visual theme for your overall presentation. The more highly developed and fine-tuned you make your presentation, the greater its impact will be on your audience.

With a large amount of the textual content already in place, you will now begin to think more about the big picture. A well-organized and professional-looking presentation will only add to your authority and credibility as a presenter.

Slide Layouts

Throughout your presentation, you will likely need to include different types of information on various slides. PowerPoint 2016 includes a selection of *slide layouts* that allow you to organize different types of content in a logical and visually appealing manner. A slide layout is a template that determines the placement of different types of content on a slide.

You can select slide layouts as you add slides to your presentation. You can also apply slide layouts to existing slides. Placeholders for items such as text, tables, charts, and images are built into the various slide layouts.

Types of Slide Layouts

PowerPoint includes nine standard slide layouts that you can add to your presentation. The following table describes each of the standard slide layouts and explains the type of content they include.

Slide Layout	What It Includes
Title Slide  Title Slide	Text placeholders for a title and a subtitle.
Title and Content Title and Content	A text placeholder for a slide title, and a content placeholder for content such as tables, images, graphs, charts, or videos.

Slide Layout	What It Includes
Section Header Section Header	Text placeholders for section and subsection titles.
Two Content Two Content	A text placeholder for a slide title, and two content placeholders for a variety of content types.
Comparison Comparison	A text placeholder for a slide title, two content placeholders for a variety of content types, and two text placeholders to title or label the two content objects.
Title Only Title Only	A text placeholder to enter a slide title.
Blank Blank	No placeholders.
Content with Caption  Content with Caption	A text placeholder for a slide title, a text placeholder for textual content, and a content placeholder for a variety of content types.

Slide Layout	What It Includes
Picture with Caption Picture with Caption	A title text placeholder, a picture placeholder, and a text placeholder for caption text.

Note: Templates can contain more than the nine standard slide layouts.

The Slide Size and Orientation Settings

In addition to selecting from the various layouts, PowerPoint 2016 gives you the ability to modify the size and the orientation of your slides. The default size of the PowerPoint slide is 13.3 inches by 7.5 inches. This is in the 16:9 aspect ratio, which is the format for high definition television broadcasts. Other sizes, such as the 4:3 standard definition format and 35mm slides, are also available. You can also switch between the default landscape orientation and portrait orientation.

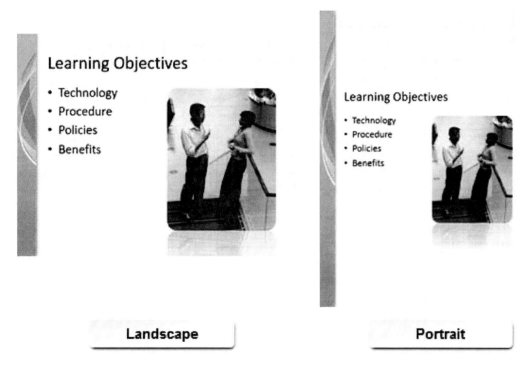

Figure 2-9: PowerPoint slides in the landscape and portrait orientations.

Note: PowerPoint Online App

When you add slides, the same slide layouts are available in the online app; however, you do not have the ability to change the slide size. To do so, you must open the presentation in PowerPoint 2016.

Access the Checklist tile on your CHOICE Course screen for reference information and job aids on How to Add, Delete, and Modify Slides.

ACTIVITY 2-3
Adding, Deleting, and Modifying Slides

Data Files

C:\091060Data\Developing a PowerPoint Presentation\Project Team.pptx

C:\091060Data\Developing a PowerPoint Presentation\Dexter_Collingsworth_Resume.docx

Before You Begin

The file My Bio Presentation.pptx is open.

The file Dexter_Collingsworth_Resume.docx is open.

Scenario

You decide you would like to add slides to introduce various sections of your presentation. You also remember that a colleague from school used a picture of you in a PowerPoint presentation that she put together for an old project. You think the image would be appropriate for your biography, so you decide to use the slide in your current presentation, and to delete the slides you will not need. In addition, you want to include slides that contain information about your work experience, education, and projects.

---

1. Reuse a slide with a picture.
   a) Navigate to slide **1**.
   b) Select **Home→Slides→New Slide** down arrow and then select **Reuse Slides**.
   c) In the **Reuse Slides** pane, select the **Browse** button, and then select **Browse File**.
   d) In the **Browse** dialog box, navigate to the **C:\091060Data\Developing a PowerPoint Presentation** folder.
   e) Select the **Project Team.pptx** file, and then select **Open**.
   f) In the **Reuse Slides** pane, select slide **2**.
   g) Select the **Close** button to close the pane.

2. Modify existing title slides.
   a) In the left pane, navigate to slide **4** titled "Training Outline."
   b) Replace the existing title text with *My Qualifications*
   c) Navigate to slide **5** and replace the existing title text with *My Experience*

3. Delete a series of slides.
   a) In the left pane, select slide **9** titled "Lesson 2: Content"
   b) Press and hold down the **Shift** key, and then select slide **12** titled "Lesson 3: Content."
   c) Press the **Delete** key.

4. Add content from the Word file.
   a) In the left pane, select slide **5**, titled "My Experience."
   b) Switch to the Word 2016 window and copy the text in the **Employment History** section.
   c) Switch to the presentation, select the existing bulleted text, and paste in the copied text to overwrite it.

5. Add a slide to the presentation after the My Experience slide.

---

a) Select **Home**→**Slides**→**New Slide** down arrow, and from the drop-down menu, select **Title and Content**.
b) Change the title text to *My Education*
c) From the Word document, copy the text in the **Education** section and paste it in the content placeholder of slide 6.

6. **Add a Projects slide to the presentation.**
   a) Add another slide to the presentation with the Title and Content layout.
   b) Change the title text to *Projects*
   c) From the Word document, copy the text in the **Projects** section and paste it in the content placeholder of slide 7.

7. **Close the Word 2016 window.**

8. **Modify slide content.**
   a) In the left pane, navigate to slide **12**.
   b) Replace the existing text with the text given in the image.

Summary

- Education
- Hands-on research and development experience
- Design team leadership

9. **Delete non-contiguous slides.**
   a) In the left pane, select slide **8** titled "Lesson 1: Content."
   b) Press and hold down the **Ctrl** key, and then select slide **9** titled "Lesson 1: Wrap-up," slide **11** titled "Lesson 3: Wrap-up," and slide **13** titled "Assessment and Evaluation."
   c) Press the **Delete** key.
   d) Save the changes to the file.

Slide Arrangement

As you develop your presentation, you may find that a different arrangement of slides makes more sense than the one you originally planned. Or, the focus of your presentation might change due to outside influence, such as a request from your supervisor or a peer. PowerPoint allows you to arrange and organize the order of your slides to suit your needs.

> **Note: PowerPoint Online App**
>
> Even though the **Slide Sorter** view is not available in the online app, you can rearrange slides by dragging them in the **Thumbnails** pane.

> Access the Checklist tile on your CHOICE Course screen for reference information and job aids on How to Arrange Slides.

ACTIVITY 2-4
Arranging Slides

Before You Begin

The file My Bio Presentation.pptx is open.

Scenario

You have finished creating the slides you will need for the presentation during the team meeting. You realize you have included all pertinent information for a brief professional biography, but you have not arranged the slides in the proper order. You will need to organize your slides in a logical manner before presenting to your new team.

1. Move a slide in the **Normal** view.
   a) In the left pane, select slide **8** titled "Today's Overview."
   b) Select **Home→Clipboard→Cut**.

    Note: You can also use the keyboard shortcut **Ctrl+X**.

   c) In the left pane, select slide **2** which has a photo.
   d) Select **Home→Clipboard→Paste**.

    Note: Observe that the subsequent slides have been moved one place down in the slide order.

2. Arrange the remaining slides in the **Slide Sorter** view.
   a) Select **View→Presentation Views→Slide Sorter**.
   b) In the **Slide Sorter** view, select slide **7** titled "My Education," and then drag and drop it in between slides **5** and **6**.
   c) Select slide **5** titled "My Qualifications."
   d) Drag and drop the slide in between slides **3** and **4**.

3. Review the order of your slides.
   a) In the **Presentation Views** group, select the **Normal** button.
   b) Navigate through the slides to ensure they are in a logical order.
      Slides 3-8 should be in the following order: **Today's Overview**, **My Qualifications**, **My Skills**, **My Education**, **My Experience**, and **Projects**.
   c) Save the file.

Themes

Themes are combinations of colors, fonts, and effects that give your presentation a consistent look and feel throughout. Themes help to define the background color of slides and the color and style of objects such as charts and tables. You can apply themes to individual slides, groups of slides, or your entire presentation.

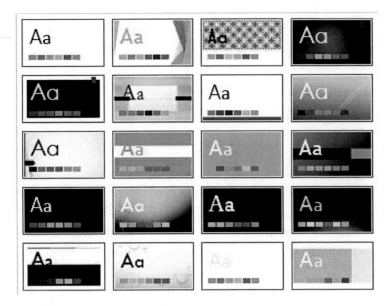

Figure 2-10: PowerPoint themes.

> **Note:** To further explore themes, you can access the LearnTO **Decide Between PowerPoint Templates and Themes** presentation from the **LearnTO** tile on the CHOICE Course screen.

Quick Styles

Quick Styles are themes that can quickly be applied to a particular object on a slide by selecting a single command button. Quick Styles are found in galleries and often appear in contextual tabs when objects such as charts or graphs are selected.

> **Note: PowerPoint Online App**
>
> You can apply themes to your presentations in the online app; however, you are not able to modify the theme components, including the fonts and effects. In addition, the Quick Styles feature is not available for every slide object. If you want to customize the theme or use Quick Styles, you must do so in PowerPoint 2016.

Theme Variants

If you happen to like many of the design elements contained in a particular theme, but you aren't quite sure it fits your needs, you can tweak the look of the theme by selecting one of its *theme variants*. Theme variants are collections of closely related themes that share many of the same layout and design elements, but with some changes. A theme variant may contain all of the same design elements of a theme, but have a different color palette. Some theme variants may change only the background of the theme. Theme variants allow you to quickly make changes to your presentation's theme without having to start from scratch or choose another theme altogether.

Theme Components

The three visual components of themes are colors, fonts, and effects. While themes contain pre-determined attributes for these components, you can customize them to suit your needs.

Theme Component	Description
Colors	Theme colors determine the color applied to particular on-slide elements. A theme contains four text and background colors, six accent colors, and two hyperlink colors. You can select from the preset color themes in PowerPoint 2016, or you can create your own custom color themes.
Fonts	Themes apply a different font to title text and the body text on slides.
Effects	Themes apply effects, such as drop shadows, reflections, and beveled edges, to on-slide elements. You cannot create a custom set of effects in PowerPoint 2016. You must choose from among the sets of included effects themes.

Background Styles

Background styles are the colors, images, or textures that make up slide backgrounds. These can be set by applying themes to your slides, or you can create custom backgrounds.

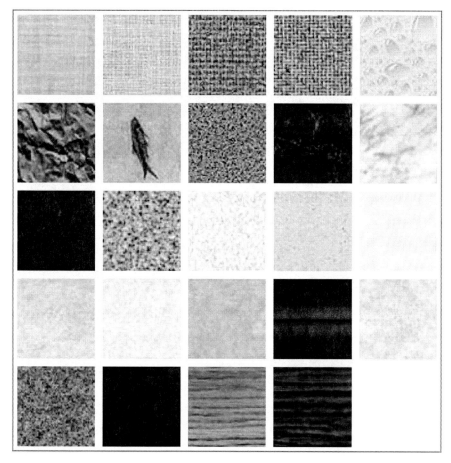

Figure 2-11: A sampling of the textured backgrounds available in PowerPoint 2016.

Hide Background Graphics

You can hide any graphics that appear in the background of a slide by using the **Hide Background Graphics** option. If you apply a theme to a presentation and the style does not appear to change on certain slides, you might need to hide background images to view the actual slide backgrounds.

 Note: Hiding background images will not hide background fills, such as textures or gradients.

The Format Background Pane

You can find options for customizing the backgrounds of slides in the **Format Background** pane. The commands on the **Format Background** pane are divided into three tabs: **Fill**, **Effects**, and **Picture**.

The available commands on the tabs will vary depending on the type of background you have selected. For example, if you do not have a picture or a textured background selected, you will not have access to the commands for adding artistic effects.

Tab Option	Allows You To
Fill	Access options for creating solid, gradient, picture or texture, and pattern fills. You can also adjust various attributes for fills, such as brightness, transparency, and color.
Effects	Apply artistic effects to background images and textures.
Picture	Adjust the attributes, such as sharpness, brightness, and contrast, of pictures that are being used as backgrounds.

> **Note: PowerPoint Online App**
>
> You can use the **Format Background** pane to change the fill but you are limited to solid colors. Likewise, you can change the background to be a picture, but it can't be customized. To make advanced customizations, you must use the desktop application.

> **Access the Checklist tile on your CHOICE Course screen for reference information and job aids on How to Work with Themes.**

ACTIVITY 2-5
Working with Themes

Before You Begin
The file My Bio Presentation.pptx is open.

Scenario
Your biography is nearly complete, but you don't like the overall look of the presentation and you would like to give it some pizazz. You decide to spruce up the original template by changing the theme and the background style.

---

1. **Apply a theme to the presentation.**
   a) Select the **Design** tab.
   b) In the **Themes** group, select the **More** button ⏷ to expand the **Themes** gallery.
   c) Select the **Retrospect** theme.

    Note: You can hover over the themes in the **Themes** gallery to find the specific theme you require.

2. **Apply a theme variant to the presentation.**
   a) On the **Design** tab, in the **Variants** group, hover the cursor over each theme variant to preview them.
   b) Select the **More** button to expand the **Variants** gallery.
   c) Select the blue theme variant, which is the first tile in the second row.

3. **Apply a gradient fill to a slide's background.**
   a) Navigate to slide **2**, which contains a photo.
   b) Select **Design→Customize→Format Background**.
   c) Expand the **Fill** section and then select the **Gradient fill** option.
   d) Select the **Preset gradients** drop-down list.
   e) From the gallery, select **Light Gradient - Accent 6**, which is the last tile in the first row.
   f) Close the **Format Background** pane.
   g) Save and close the file.

Summary

In this lesson, you began developing a PowerPoint presentation. You selected a presentation type, viewed and navigated a presentation, edited text, and built a presentation. Now that you have a solid understanding of the basic functions of PowerPoint 2016, you are ready to begin exploring its more advanced features.

How can customizing presentations help you convey your thoughts and ideas more effectively?

As you have worked with PowerPoint 2016, have you discovered alternate methods for performing some of the functions covered in this training? Is this similar to your experience with other Microsoft Office applications?

 Note: Check your CHOICE Course screen for opportunities to interact with your classmates, peers, and the larger CHOICE online community about the topics covered in this course or other topics you are interested in. From the Course screen you can also access available resources for a more continuous learning experience.

3 Performing Advanced Text Editing Operations

Lesson Time: 50 minutes

Lesson Introduction

You have begun developing Microsoft® Office PowerPoint® 2016 presentations with strong visual appeal and a consistent look and feel. You have mastered the basic building blocks of presentations, and you know how to customize your presentations to suit your particular needs. Now, you will focus on honing your message by utilizing some of the advanced text editing features in PowerPoint 2016.

Not all content carries the same weight. You will need ways to emphasize certain key points, while still presenting all relevant information to your audience. Additionally, you may want to format the text in your presentations to make it easier to read or to have more visual appeal. But, none of this should consume large amounts of your development time. By becoming familiar with some of the advanced text editing features in PowerPoint 2016, you will be able to focus on your message instead of wasting hours of time customizing the appearance of your text.

Lesson Objectives

In this lesson, you will:

- Format characters.
- Format paragraphs.
- Format text boxes.

TOPIC A

Format Characters

Text is likely to be one of your main means of conveying information. As such, it is important to select the best character formatting for your presentations. The proper character formatting will give your presentation a professional appearance while ensuring that the audience does not miss out on key information.

Without formatting, the text in your presentations will appear flat. There will be no visual cues for the audience to interpret the text, and the presentation will be just plain boring. You have entered text into your presentations, now you will energize that text.

Character Formats

Character formats are particular attributes that you can apply to the text on your slides. By changing these attributes, you can alter the appearance of the text in your presentation. There are four basic elements of character formats: font type, size, color, and style.

> **Note: PowerPoint Online App**
>
> You can modify the font type, font size, and font color of selected text by using the buttons on the ribbon or the **Mini** toolbar. For additional styles, you are limited to applying bold, italics, and underline to text. The advanced formatting features that are covered in the remainder of this topic are only available in PowerPoint 2016.

Clear All Formatting

The **Clear All Formatting** option enables you to reset any formatting you applied to text.

The Font Dialog Box

The **Font** dialog box provides advanced character formatting options to customize the text in your presentations. These options enable you to format individual characters and adjust the spacing between them.

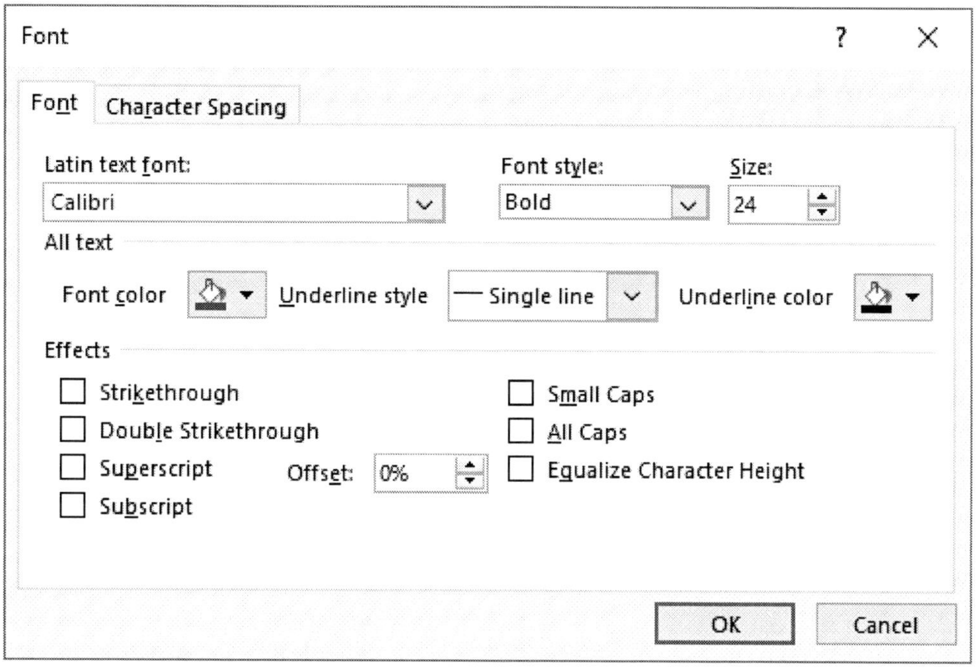

Figure 3-1: Character formatting options in the Font dialog box.

The following table describes the **Font** dialog box options.

Font Dialog Box Option	Description
Latin text font	Allows you to select from any of the included font types in PowerPoint 2016.
Font style	Allows you to select a font style, such as bold, italic, bold italic, or regular.
Size	Allows you to modify the size of text on your slides.
Font color	Opens a gallery of text color options. The **More Colors** option enables you to customize the color of the text in your presentations.
Underline style	Allows you to select a style of underline for emphasizing text.
Underline color	Allows you to select a color for your underlines. You can also customize underline colors.
Effects	Provides a selection of additional textual effects including Strikethrough, All Caps, Superscript, Subscript, and Equalize Character Height. You can also specify the offset percentage for superscript and subscript.
Character Spacing Tab	Provides options for adjusting the spacing between textual characters.

Note: Many of the commands in the **Font** dialog box can be accessed via buttons on the ribbon.

WordArt Styles

WordArt styles are predetermined formatting configurations that can be applied to text on a slide. These formatting configurations can be applied to selected text or to all text within a text placeholder. The **WordArt Styles** gallery, enables you to preview different WordArt styles and apply them to text.

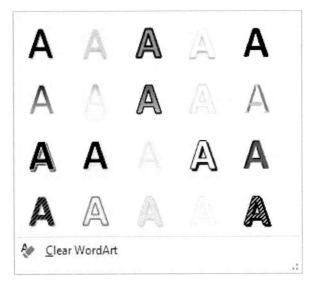

Figure 3-2: The WordArt styles gallery.

The Format Painter Tool

The *Format Painter* tool allows you to copy the formatting of selected text and apply it to other text. It functions much like the copy and paste commands, however, only the formatting, and not the text, is copied.

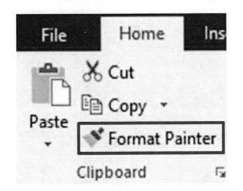

Figure 3-3: The Format Painter tool on the ribbon.

The Replace Font Option

The *Replace Font* option allows you to easily change all text of a particular font type to another font type throughout an entire presentation. This option can come in handy when you create your presentation on one computer, and then deliver your presentation from another. If the fonts you created your project with don't exist on the computer you deliver your presentation from, this feature can be a lifesaver. The **Replace Font** dialog box provides options that enable you to specify the fonts to be replaced.

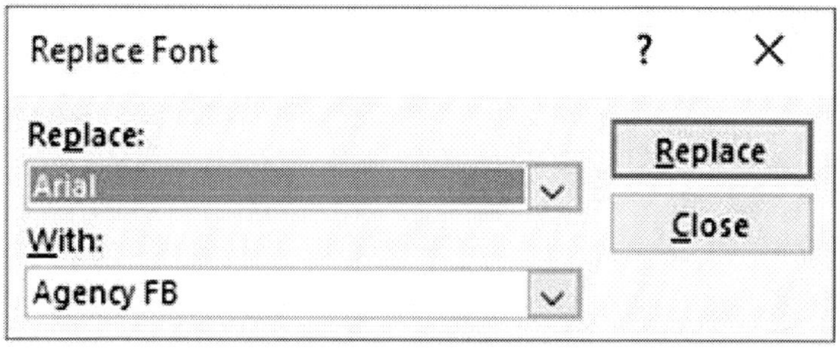

Figure 3-4: The Replace Font dialog box with options to specify the required fonts.

Access the Checklist tile on your CHOICE Course screen for reference information and job aids on How to Format Characters.

ACTIVITY 3-1
Formatting Characters

Data File

C:\091060Data\Performing Advanced Text Editing Operations\Bio_Editing.pptx

Scenario

You have applied some thematic elements to your presentation that have made some of the text difficult to read. You decide to change the text formatting to make your presentation easier to read.

1. Change the font style of selected text.
   a) From the **C:\091060Data\Performing Advanced Text Editing Operations** folder, open the **Bio_Editing.pptx** file.
   b) In the left pane, navigate to slide **5**.
   c) Select all of the text in the first bullet point.
   d) On the **Home** tab, in the **Font** group, from the **Font** drop-down list, select **Arial**.
   e) Click outside the text box to deselect it.

2. Replace fonts in the presentation.
   a) Select **Home→Editing→Replace** down arrow, and then select **Replace Fonts**.

   b) In the **Replace Font** dialog box, from the **Replace** drop-down list, select **Trebuchet MS**.
   c) From the **With** drop-down list, select **Arial**.
   d) Select **Replace** to replace the fonts, and then select **Close**.

   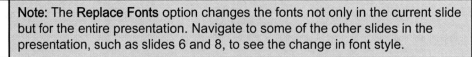

   > **Note:** The **Replace Fonts** option changes the fonts not only in the current slide but for the entire presentation. Navigate to some of the other slides in the presentation, such as slides 6 and 8, to see the change in font style.

3. Change the color of the text.
   a) Navigate to slide **2** and select the text "Dexter Collingsworth."
   b) On the **Mini** toolbar, select the **Font Color** down arrow. **A ▾**
   c) From the **Theme Colors** menu, select **Black, Background 1**, which is the first color.
   d) Navigate to slide **5**.
   e) In the first bullet point, select all of the text.
   f) On the **Mini** toolbar, select the **Font Color** button.

   > **Note:** Selecting the **Font Color** button applies black color to the text. This is because you selected black in an earlier step and black color remains as the current selection in the **Font Color** button.

4. Format text by using the **Format Painter** tool.

   a) On the **Home** tab, in the **Clipboard** group, double-click **Format Painter**.

   > **Note:** Double-clicking the **Format Painter** button activates sticky mode.

   b) Select all of the text in the second bullet point to apply the formatting you copied using the **Format Painter** tool.

   c) Similarly, use the **Format Painter** tool to apply the same formatting to the third bullet point.

   d) Select **Home→Clipboard→Format Painter**.

5. Apply WordArt to the title text.

   a) Navigate to slide **1**.

   b) Select the "My Bio" title text.

   c) On the **Drawing Tools** contextual tab, select the **Format** tab.

   d) In the **WordArt Styles** group, select the **More** button ⟱ to display the **WordArt Style** gallery.

   e) Select the **Fill - Orange, Accent 1, Outline 1 - Background 1, Hard Shadow - Accent 1** WordArt style, which is the third tile in the third row.

   f) Click anywhere outside the text box to deselect it.

6. Save the file in the **C:\091060Data\Performing Advanced Text Editing Operations** folder as *My Bio Edited.pptx*

TOPIC B

Format Paragraphs

Formatting and applying styles to your text can make your presentation easier to read and can help you convey your message. But, there is another important aspect of organizing and formatting your textual content: formatting paragraphs. Now that you have tailored your text to have just the right look, you will organize the physical layout of your text by formatting your paragraphs.

The paragraph formatting options in PowerPoint 2016 give you the ability to control the overall layout of the text in your presentations. Think of paragraph formatting as how you organize the structure of your textual content.

Bulleted Lists

Bulleted lists are used to display a sequence of items for which the order is not important. Each of the items displays as a line of text with an image, or a bullet, to the left. PowerPoint 2016 allows you to add bulleted lists to your textual content and provides a number of options for formatting them. You can select the appearance of the bullets in your lists, create custom bullets, create bulleted lists with multiple sub-levels, and alter the distance between the margin of the text placeholder and the bullet items in your lists.

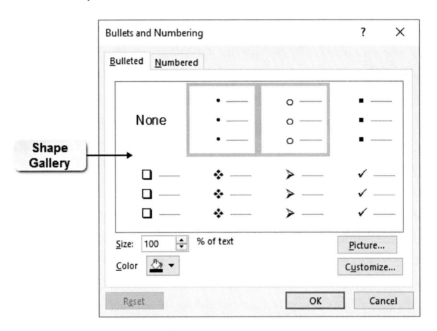

Figure 3-5: Bulleted list formatting options in the Bullets and Numbering dialog box.

The **Bullets and Numbering** dialog box provides several options to format bulleted lists.

Option	Allows You To
Shape Gallery	Select from the default PowerPoint bullet shapes: filled round, hollow round, filled square, hollow square, star, arrow, or check mark.
Size	Set the size of the bullets as a percentage of the size of the text.
Color	Change the color of the bullets in your bulleted lists. This does not change the color of the text in your list.

Option	Allows You To
Picture	Import an image to use as bullets.
Customize	Select a symbol to use as bullets.

> **Note: PowerPoint Online App**
>
> You can apply simple bullets or numbering to selected paragraphs. The **Bullets and Numbering** dialog box is not available in the online app. If you want to customize the style of either the bullets or numbering, you will need to do so in PowerPoint 2016.

Numbered Lists

Use numbered lists to display a series of items for which the order is important, for example, the steps in a process or procedure. As with bulleted lists, PowerPoint 2016 provides you with a number of options for formatting your numbered lists. You can use Arabic or Roman numerals in your numbered lists, as well as letters. This can be useful for presenting high-level outlines to your audience.

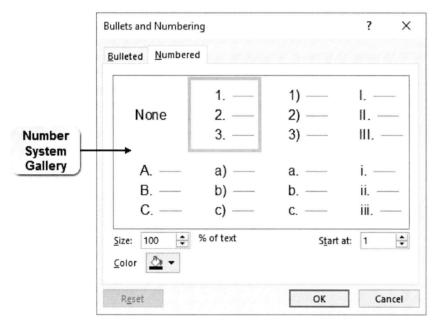

Figure 3-6: Numbered list formatting options in the Bullets and Numbering dialog box.

The **Bullets and Numbering** dialog box provides several options to format numbered lists.

Option	Allows You To
Number System Gallery	Select from among Arabic numerals, Roman numerals, and letters for your numbered lists.
Size	Set the font size of the numbers or letters as a percentage of the size of the text.
Color	Change the color of the numbers or letters in your numbered list. This does not change the color of the list text.
Start At	Specify the initial number or letter value to begin your numbered lists.

Note: You can also apply bullets or numbering to existing paragraph text. All text separated by a line break will become an individual bullet or numbered item.

Access the Checklist tile on your CHOICE Course screen for reference information and job aids on How to Use Bulleted and Numbered Lists.

ACTIVITY 3-2
Using Bulleted and Numbered Lists

Before You Begin
The file My Bio Edited.pptx is open.

Scenario
You have formatted the text characters in your presentation. You feel the text is easier to read, but you aren't happy with the way the bullets look. So, you decide to change the formatting of the bulleted lists.

1. **Change the bullet style for the list in the fifth slide.**
   a) Navigate to slide **5**, and then select all of the bulleted list text on the slide.
   b) Select **Home→Paragraph→Bullets** down arrow.
   c) From the drop-down menu, select **Bullets and Numbering** to display the **Bullets and Numbering** dialog box.
   d) On the **Bulleted** tab, select **Star Bullets**, which is the second bullet style in the second row.
   e) Select **OK**.

2. **Modify the bullet size.**
   a) Display the **Bullets and Numbering** dialog box.
   b) On the **Bulleted** tab, in the **Size** field, use the spin buttons to change the bullet size to **150** percent of the text.

    Note: Notice that the bullets now are bigger than the text. Most of the time, you'll want to avoid this in your presentation. This step is meant to make it easier for you to see the change in formatting.

   c) Select **OK**.

3. **Change bullets to a numbered list.**
   a) Navigate to slide **9**.
   b) Select all of the bulleted list text on the slide.
   c) Select the **Home→Paragraph→Numbering** button.
   d) Save the file.

Text Alignment Options

PowerPoint offers you several options for horizontally aligning the text within text placeholders and other objects. The text alignment options allow you to position text relative to the left and right margins within the text box or object.

Option	Result
Align Left ≡	Text is lined up along the left margin.
Center ≡	Text is centered evenly between the left and right margins.

Option	Result
Align Right ≡	Text is lined up along the right margin.
Justify ≡	Text is left-aligned. Additionally, extra spaces between words or characters may be added to square off the text block, providing a uniform look along the left and right edges.
Add or Remove Columns ≣▾	Creates individual columns for text. Up to 16 columns are available in a text box.

> **Note:** As with bullets and numbered lists, you can adjust the margins of text by using the **Decrease List Level** or **Increase List Level** buttons.

> **Note: PowerPoint Online App**
>
> You can use the four basic paragraph alignment styles: **Align Left**, **Center**, **Align Right**, and **Justify**. All other advanced alignment styles must be applied using PowerPoint 2016.

Vertical Text Alignment Options

PowerPoint 2016 also provides you three options for vertically aligning your text. The vertical text alignment options allow you to position the text relative to the top and bottom margins within the text box or object.

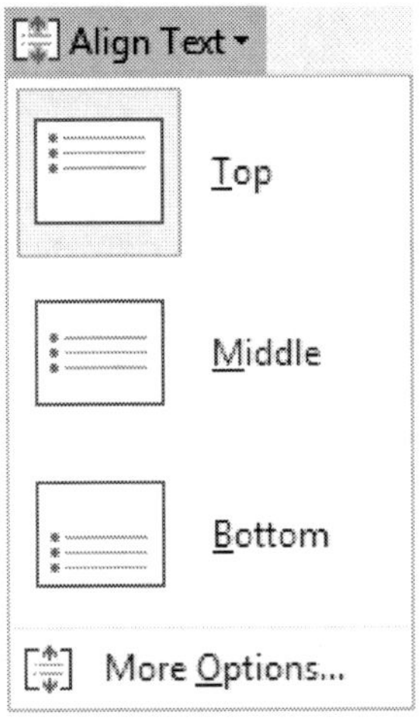

Figure 3-7: Vertical text alignment options.

The following table describes the vertical text alignment options.

Option	Text Is
Top	Vertically aligned along the top of the text box.
Middle	Centered vertically.
Bottom	Vertically aligned along the bottom of the text box.

The Format Shape Pane

The **Format Shape** pane contains most of the commands you can use to format objects, such as text boxes, as well as the text within the objects. While many of the commands in the **Format**

Shape pane are available from the ribbon, some commands can be accessed only from the **Format Shape** pane.

The **Format Shape** pane is divided into two sections, **Shape Options** and **Text Options**, both of which are divided into tabs that contain the various commands.

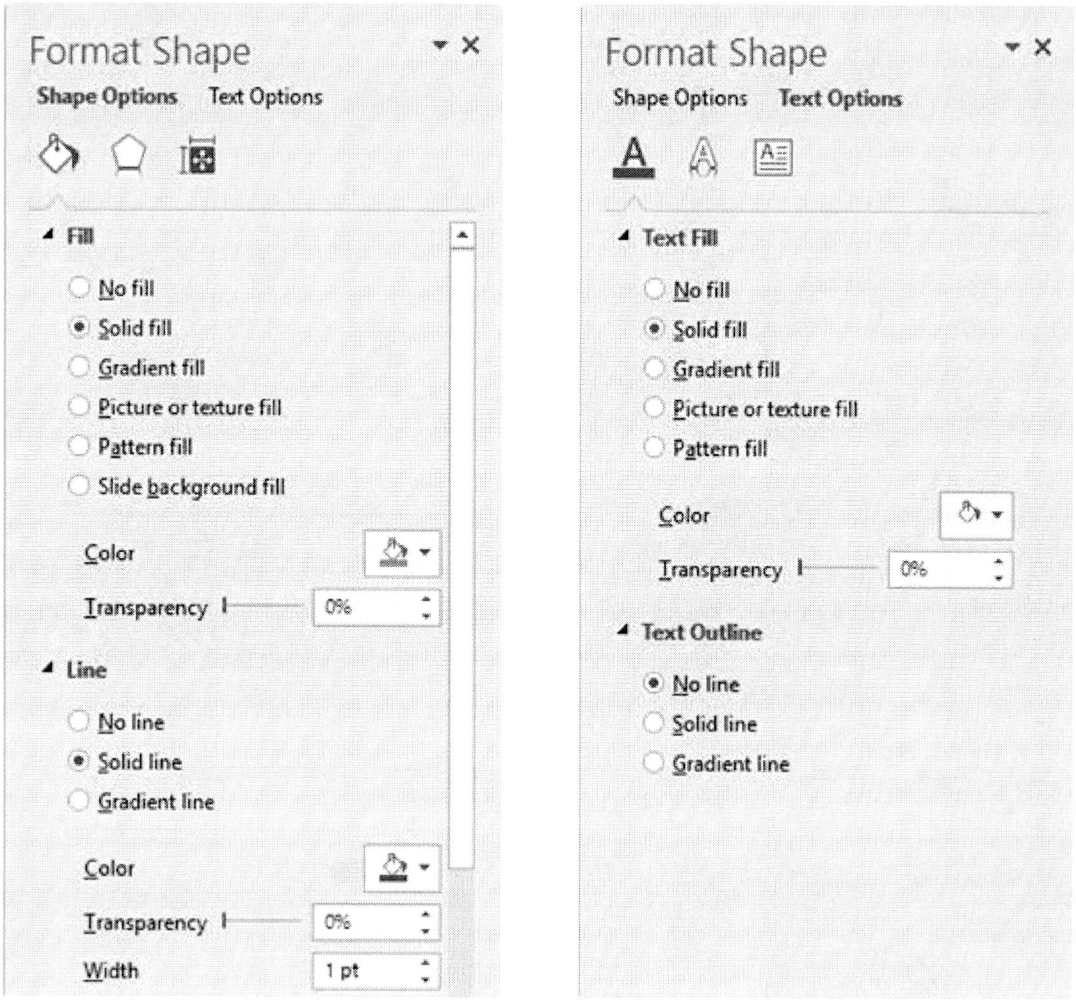

Figure 3-8: The Shape Options and the Text Options sections of the Format Shape pane.

The Shape Options Tab Commands

The **Shape Options** tab contains the commands you will use to format text boxes and other on-slide objects.

Shape Options Tab	Contains Commands For
Fill & Line	Modifying the outline and the background of objects.
Effects	Applying shadows, reflections, 3D rotation, and other effects to objects.
Size & Properties	Determining the size and location of objects, and for formatting paragraphs within objects.
Picture	Modifying and applying image attributes.

The Text Options Tab Commands

The **Text Options** tab contain the commands you will use to format the text within text boxes and other objects.

Text Options Tab	Contains Commands For
Text Fill & Outline A	Modifying and customizing the text fill color and outline.
Text Effects A	Applying shadows, reflections, 3D rotation, and other effects to text.
Text Box A≡	Aligning text within objects and selecting Autofit options.

Note: PowerPoint Online App

The **Format Shape** pane is not available in the online app; however, you can modify the shape fill and outline by using the buttons in the **Drawing** group on the **HOME** tab. To apply advanced formatting options, you must open the presentation in PowerPoint 2016.

The Autofit Feature

The *Autofit feature* gives you options for automatically fitting text within text boxes and other objects regardless of how much text you enter. The options in the **Format Shape** pane enable you to specify the Autofit setting for a text box or object. The default Autofit setting is **Resize shape to fit text**.

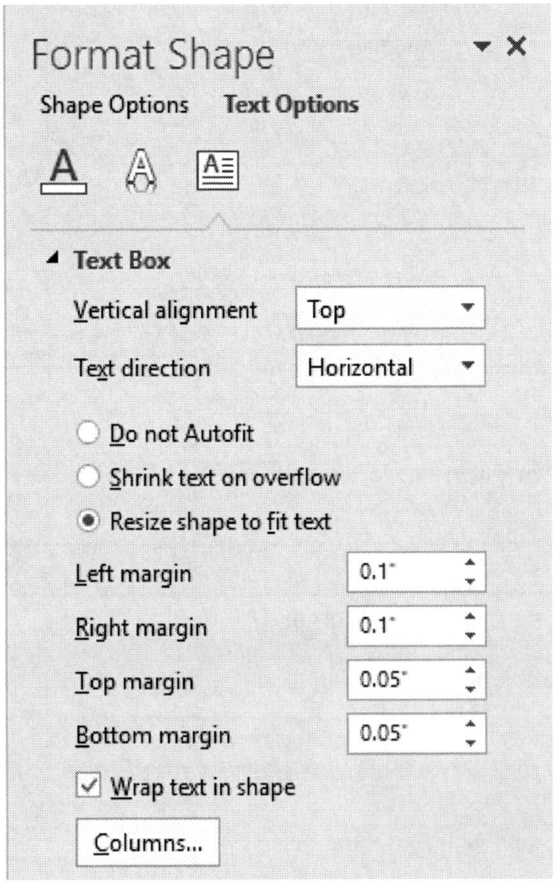

Figure 3-9: The Autofit commands on the Format Shape pane.

The following table describes the Autofit feature options.

Option	Effect
Do not Autofit	PowerPoint will adjust neither the text nor the text box. If you enter more text than will fit in a text box, the extra text will spill over and appear outside the text box.
Shrink text on overflow	PowerPoint will automatically decrease the size of the text if you enter more text than will fit.
Resize shape to fit text	PowerPoint will automatically increase the size of the text box if you enter more text than will fit.

Note: When the **Do not Autofit** option is selected, any text that spills over off of the text box is still associated with the text box. While the text appears outside the border, changes made to the text box will affect the overflowing text. For example, if you move the text box, the text will move with it. If you delete the text box, you will also delete the overflowing text.

Note: PowerPoint Online App

This feature is not available in the online app. To apply advanced formatting options, you must open the presentation in PowerPoint 2016.

Wrap Text in Shape

When the **Wrap text in shape** check box in the **Format Shape** pane is checked, text entered into shapes will align to the edges of the shape.

Paragraph Spacing Options

Spacing refers to the vertical distance between lines of text or paragraphs. There are three spacing attributes that can be adjusted in PowerPoint 2016: **Line Spacing**, **Before**, and **After**. The **Paragraph** dialog box enables you to specify the settings for these options.

Paragraph	? ✕
Indents and Spacing	

General

Alignment: Left ⌄

Indentation

Before text: 0.25″ Special: Hanging ⌄ By: 0.2″

Spacing

Before: 5.28 pt Line Spacing: Multiple ⌄ At: 1.25

After: 3 pt

Tabs... OK Cancel

Figure 3-10: The options in the Paragraph dialog box.

The following table describes the **Paragraph** dialog box options.

Spacing Option	Enables You to Adjust
Line Spacing	The spacing between lines of text.
Before	Text spacing by adding space before a paragraph.
After	Text spacing by adding space after a paragraph.

> **Note: PowerPoint Online App**
>
> This feature is not available in the online app. To modify the paragraph spacing options, you must open the presentation in PowerPoint 2016.

Text Direction Options

In addition to being able to format, align, and space your text, PowerPoint 2016 also gives you the ability to change the direction in which your text flows. The default text direction option is horizontal, but you can also rotate your text or stack it vertically.

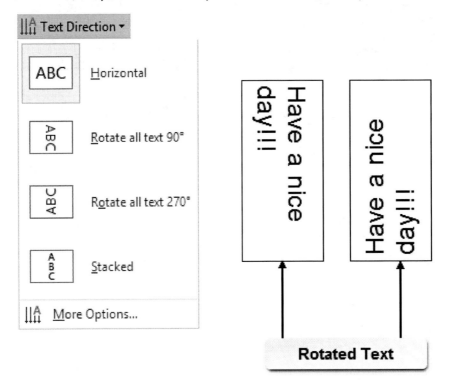
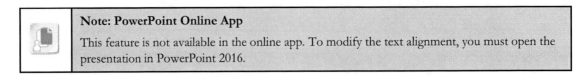

Figure 3-11: The Text Direction options in PowerPoint and their effect on text.

> **Note: PowerPoint Online App**
>
> This feature is not available in the online app. To modify the text alignment, you must open the presentation in PowerPoint 2016.

Rulers

Rulers are visual reference tools that allow you to accurately position objects on a slide. The rulers display marked increments that make it easy for you to place objects with precision. You can also use the rulers to adjust margins and indentations of text within objects.

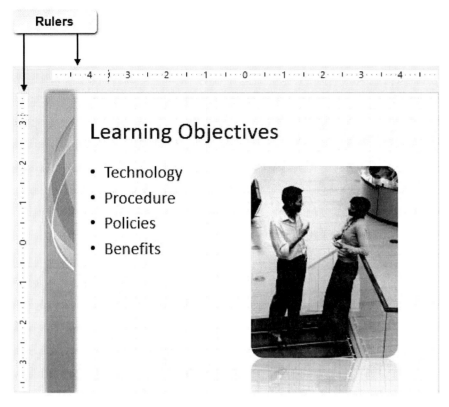

Figure 3-12: Rulers in the slide pane.

Note: PowerPoint Online App

Rulers are not available in the online app; however, they are available in PowerPoint 2016.

Access the Checklist tile on your CHOICE Course screen for reference information and job aids on How to Format Paragraphs.

ACTIVITY 3-3
Formatting Paragraphs

Before You Begin
The My Bio Edited.pptx file is open.

Scenario
You formatted the text and lists in your presentation, but you are not happy with some of the text spacing on your slides. You decide to format some of the paragraphs in your presentation to give the text a well-balanced look.

1. **Modify the horizontal text alignment.**
   a) Navigate to slide **2**.
   b) Select the "Dexter Collingsworth" text in the text box.

   c) Select **Home→Paragraph→Center.** ≡

2. **Modify the vertical text alignment.**
   a) Navigate to slide **6**.
   b) Select all of the text in the bulleted list.
   c) Select **Home→Paragraph→Align Text→Middle**.

3. **Modify the line spacing option.**

   a) Select **Home→Paragraph→Line Spacing** ‡≡ ˅ and from the drop-down menu, select **1.5** .
   b) Click outside the text box to deselect it.

4. **Modify the indentation of the text.**
   a) If necessary, on the **View** tab, in the **Show** group, check the **Ruler** check box.
   b) Select all of the text in the bulleted list.
   c) Drag the **Hanging Indent** marker to the right until it is pointing at the 1/2 inch mark on the top ruler.

d) Click outside the text box to deselect it.

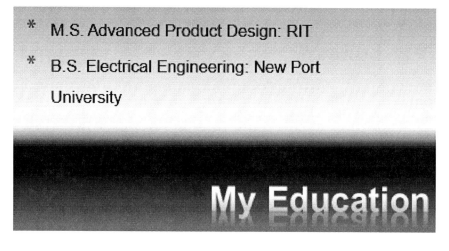

e) Save the changes to the file.

TOPIC C

Format Text Boxes

You have selected the perfect text and have it arranged on your slides just the way you like it. But, something still seems a bit dull about the way your text looks on screen, and you'd like to spruce it up a bit more. PowerPoint 2016 gives you the option of formatting the text boxes in your presentation by adding color, modifying the borders, or applying a number of effects.

Adding a little style to the text boxes in your presentation can give your textual content that added boost to keep the audience engaged. Text box formatting gives you the ability to add variety to your text and set it off from other on-slide elements. This draws the audience's attention where you want it, on your key points.

Text Placeholder Formatting Options

There are three general categories of text placeholder formatting options: fill, outline, and effects. Formatting options for text boxes, text placeholders, and shapes are the same. In addition to these options, you can quickly apply preset styles to text boxes, through the **Quick Styles** gallery.

> **Note:** You can use the **Format Painter** tool to copy and paste text box formatting as well as text formatting.

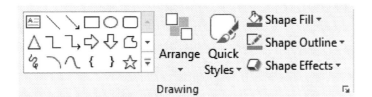

Figure 3-13: Text placeholder formatting options.

> **Note:** Inserting and working with shapes will be covered in a later lesson.

Shape Fills

As with slide backgrounds, you can add fills to the text boxes in your presentations. The **Shape Fill** drop-down menu provides you with options for adding colors, pictures, gradient fills, and textures as backgrounds for your text boxes.

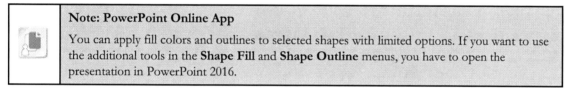

Figure 3-14: Shape Fill options.

	Note: PowerPoint Online App
	You can apply fill colors and outlines to selected shapes with limited options. If you want to use the additional tools in the **Shape Fill** and **Shape Outline** menus, you have to open the presentation in PowerPoint 2016.

The Eyedropper Tool

The *Eyedropper* is a tool that is displayed in several menus in PowerPoint 2016. You can use the **Eyedropper** tool to apply color to objects based on the color of another on-slide element. Let's say there is an image on one of your slides with a color you feel would work well as a text box border. You can use the **Eyedropper** tool to capture that color from the image and apply it to your text box borders. The **Eyedropper** tool works on a number of different objects in PowerPoint.

Shape Outlines

Text boxes are objects that are contained within a slide. As such, they have borders, or outlines, to separate them from other content on the slide. PowerPoint gives you an array of options for formatting the outlines of text boxes and other shapes.

Option	Allows You To
Color	Select the color of the outline.
No Outline	Remove the outline.
Weight	Set the line width of the outline.
Dashes	Select from among various styles of dashed lines for the outline.

Shape Effects

PowerPoint 2016 allows you to select from a variety of effects for text boxes and shapes, such as beveled or soft edges, 3-D rotation, and the addition of drop shadows. Each type of effect has an associated gallery with pre-formatted options. You can also customize the effects to suit your needs. The **Shape Effects** gallery displays the pre-formatted effects.

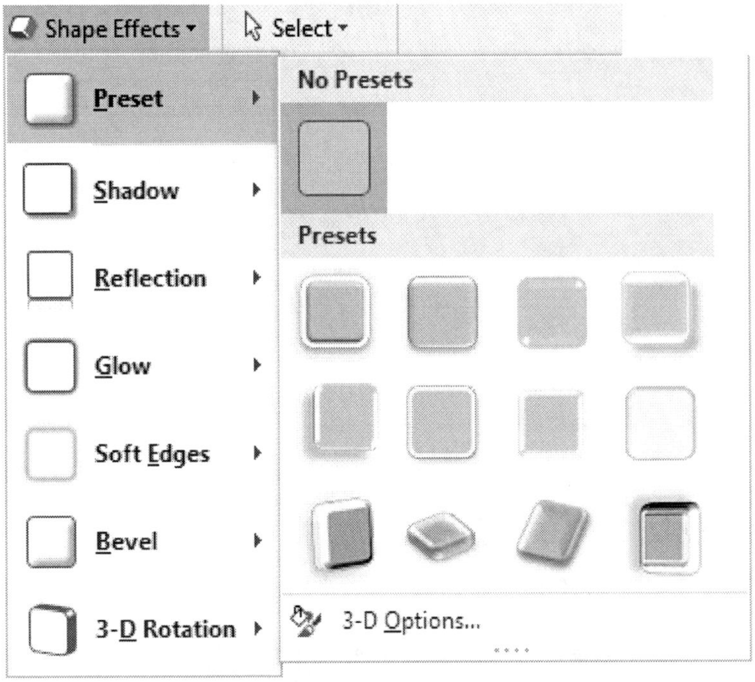

Figure 3-15: The Presets category of the Shape Effects gallery.

	Note: PowerPoint Online App This feature is not available in the online app; however, you can apply shape effects in PowerPoint 2016.

	Access the Checklist tile on your CHOICE Course screen for reference information and job aids on How to Format Text Boxes.

ACTIVITY 3-4
Formatting Text Boxes

Before You Begin
The My Bio Edited.pptx file is open.

Scenario
You have finished formatting the paragraphs in your presentation. Although you are happy with the overall look of the text, you feel the text boxes could look better. You decide to format some of the text boxes to give your presentation a more well-polished look.

1. Add a fill to a text box.
   a) If necessary, navigate to slide **5**.
   b) Select the text box with the bulleted list.

    Note: Ensure that the text box is selected and its border appears as a solid line.

   c) Select **Home→Drawing→Shape Fill**.
   d) From the drop-down menu, in the **Theme Colors** section, select a light blue color.
   e) Select **Home→Drawing→Shape Fill**.
   f) From the drop-down menu, select **Gradient** to display the **Gradient** gallery.
   g) Select the **Linear Diagonal - Top Left to Bottom Right** gradient, which is the first item in the first row.

2. Modify the fill options.
   a) On the **Home** tab, in the **Drawing** group, select the dialog box launcher to display the **Format Shape** pane.

   b) If necessary, select the **Shape Options** section, and then select the **Fill & Line** tab.
   c) Expand the **Fill** section.
   d) In the **Fill** section, drag each gradient stop to the left or to the right to adjust the gradient fill.

   Note: Each gradient stop affects only its shade of color in the gradient fill. All of the settings in the **Gradient stops** section affect only the selected gradient stop.

3. Format the outline of the text box.
   a) In the **Format Shape** pane, collapse the **Fill** section.
   b) Expand the **Line** section.
   c) In the **Line** section, select the **Solid line** option.
   d) Select the **Color** button.

    e) From the drop-down menu, in the **Theme Colors** section, select a dark red color.

 Note: A solid border appears around the text box because it is in the selected state. You may not be able to see some of the formatting you apply to the text box due to this border.

    f) In the **Width** field, use the spin box buttons to set the outline width to **3 pt**.

4. Apply an effect to the text box.

    a) In the **Format Shape** pane, select the **Effects** tab ⬠ and then expand the **Shadow** section.
    b) Select the **Presets** button to display the **Shadow** gallery.
    c) In the **Perspective** section, select **Perspective Diagonal Upper Left**, which is the first tile in that section.

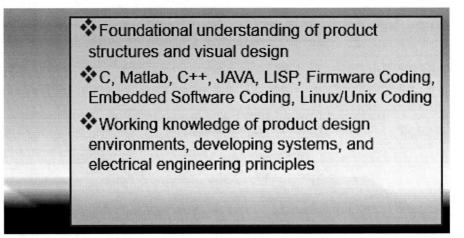

    d) Close the **Format Shape** pane.

5. Apply the same text box formats to text boxes in other slides.
    a) If necessary, select the text box with the bulleted list.
    b) On the **Home** tab, in the **Clipboard** group, double-click **Format Painter**.
    c) Navigate to slide **8** and select the text box with the bulleted list.
    d) Similarly, navigate to slide **10** and select the text box with the bulleted list.
    e) Select **Home→Clipboard→Format Painter**.

6. Save the changes and close the file.

Summary

In this lesson, you formatted text characters, paragraphs, and text boxes. Your text is now well organized and easy to read. Perhaps most importantly, your text will grab the audience's attention and focus it on the key points of your message.

How can you use the text editing and formatting features in PowerPoint 2016 to help convey your message?

Which of the text editing and formatting features do you find most useful?

 Note: Check your CHOICE Course screen for opportunities to interact with your classmates, peers, and the larger CHOICE online community about the topics covered in this course or other topics you are interested in. From the Course screen you can also access available resources for a more continuous learning experience.

4 | Adding Graphical Elements to Your Presentation

Lesson Time: 30 minutes

Lesson Introduction

You are now able to create and organize your presentation. You can also use the powerful Microsoft® Office PowerPoint® 2016 text editing features to drive your point home. But text isn't the only way to convey information to your audience. Sometimes, a picture can tell the story better than words ever could. And, graphics have the ability to keep an audience engaged and focused on what you have to say. PowerPoint 2016 gives you the ability to add a variety of graphical content to liven up your presentation.

Graphics and images are effective for illustrating concepts and processes that may be difficult to explain otherwise. The use of photos can help place your audience in a different environment to understand events from around the world. Becoming familiar with the various methods of adding graphical content in PowerPoint will give you a whole new set of options for telling your story and keeping your audience excited about what you have to say.

Lesson Objectives

In this lesson, you will:

- Insert images.
- Insert shapes.

TOPIC A

Insert Images

You will likely use some types of graphical elements more than others. For example, screenshots from a software application can be helpful in demonstrating how to accomplish a particular task. Also, there are common concepts, such as money or technology, that you may need to discuss. Quick access to images and the ability to share your computer screen will help you convey information to the audience without filling slide after slide with large amounts of text.

PowerPoint 2016 has a number of built-in graphics features that you can use to make your point. Using on-screen graphics gets your message across quickly to an audience that will, likely, not have a lot of time to review excessive textual content. And, nothing makes a presentation less engaging than lengthy, hard-to-read text.

Pictures

Pictures are the most basic form of graphical content that you can add to your PowerPoint presentation. Nearly any type of image file that you can store on your hard drive can be inserted into a slide. The **Insert Picture** dialog box enables you to insert images into your presentation.

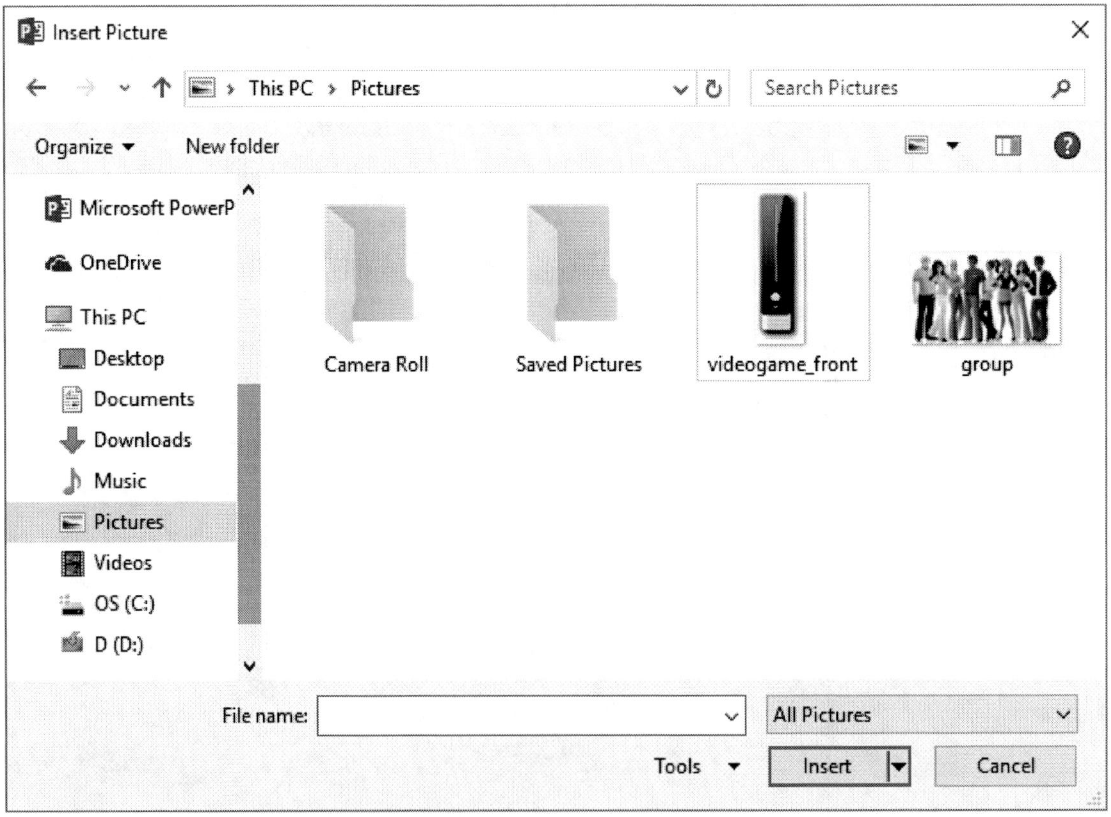

Figure 4-1: The Insert Picture dialog box.

> **Note: PowerPoint Online App**
>
> Using the **INSERT** tab, you can insert pictures and online pictures into your online presentations. You must use PowerPoint 2016 to insert pictures with the **Screenshot** and **Photo Album** tools discussed in this topic.

The Online Pictures Command

In addition to being able to add images stored on your computer to your presentations, PowerPoint 2016 allows you to insert images you can find online. The **Online Pictures** command displays the **Insert Pictures** window that provides options to search for images on the web using Bing® Image Search feature. From the web search results, you can download the image you need and insert it into your presentation. Depending on how you plan to use the images, you may be required to obtain specific licenses to use images in your presentation. You should check on the license requirement for an image before you use it.

If you have a Microsoft Account, you can also search for and insert images that you have saved in your OneDrive® folder. Additionally, you can download and insert pictures from your Facebook and Flickr® accounts.

> **Note:** Microsoft Accounts and cloud storage are covered in greater detail in the *Microsoft® Office PowerPoint® 2016: Part 2* course.

Insert Pictures

Bing Image Search
Search the web

laptops

Sign in with your Microsoft account to insert photos and videos from Facebook, Flickr, and other sites.

Figure 4-2: The Insert Pictures window with options to search for pictures online and insert them in a presentation.

> **Note:** PowerPoint 2016 does not have a specific online **Clip Art** gallery. However, you can search for Clip Art images in the **Insert Pictures** window by adding the text "clip art" to your keyword search.

The Screenshot Tool

The **Screenshot** tool gives you the ability to add anything displayed on your computer screen as an image in PowerPoint. This tool displays a gallery of windows that are available for capture. You can either insert an image of an entire window or capture a specific region using the **Screen Clipping** option.

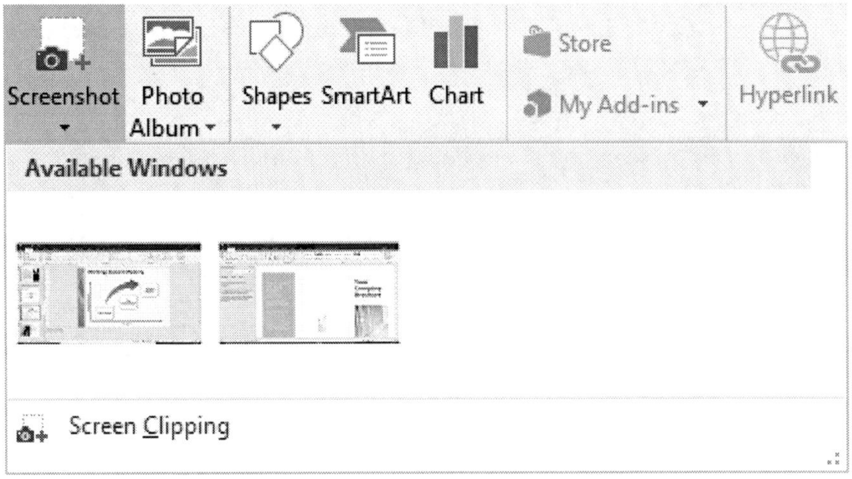

Figure 4-3: Available windows displayed in the Screenshot tool.

Note: Only windows that are not minimized to the task bar appear in the **Available Windows** pane. If you wish to insert a screen capture of your desktop, you must use the **Screen Clipping** option.

Note: To further explore the screenshot tool, you can access the LearnTO **Use the PowerPoint Screenshot Tool** presentation from the **LearnTO** tile on the CHOICE Course screen.

The Photo Album Feature

The *Photo Album feature* allows you to insert and display photographs in a custom presentation that looks like a photo album. PowerPoint 2016 provides you with the capability to add transitions, backgrounds, layouts, themes, and captions to your photo albums. You can also share your photo albums as attachments, as web publications, or in printed form.

The **Photo Album** dialog box allows you to insert photos into an album, add captions to photos, and modify the photo album layout. You can also apply effects to the images in your photo albums, such as converting images to black and white, adjusting the brightness or contrast, rotating images, and adding frames.

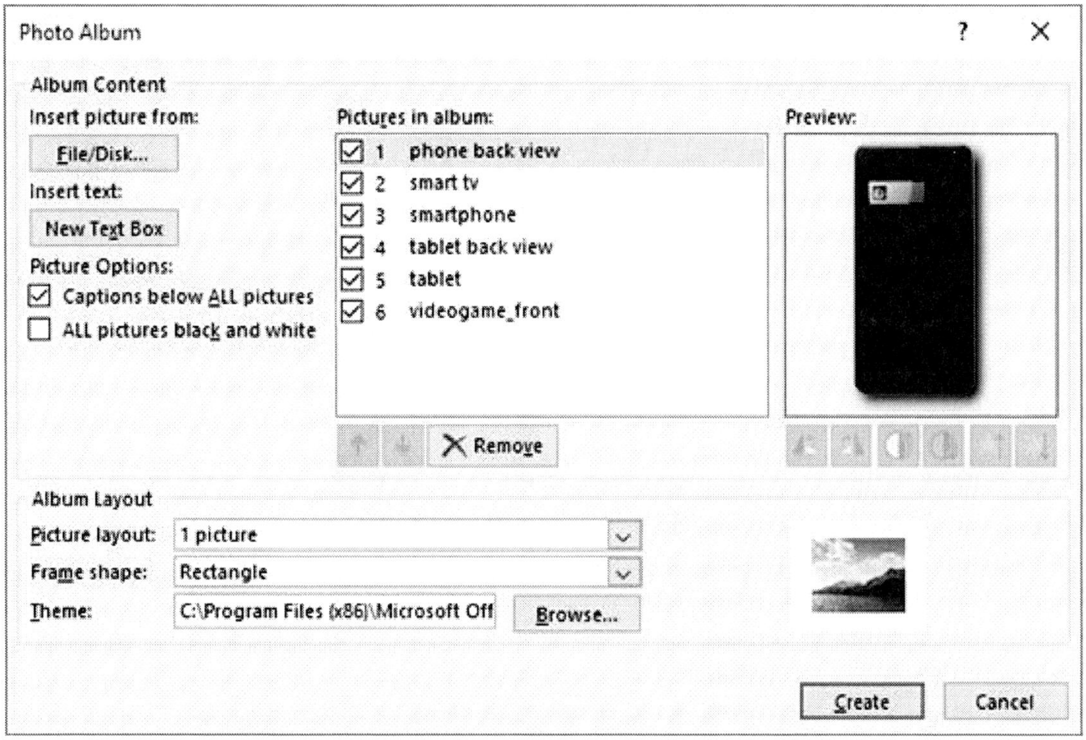

Figure 4-4: The options in the Photo Album dialog box.

Access the Checklist tile on your CHOICE Course screen for reference information and job aids on How to Insert Images into a Presentation.

ACTIVITY 4–1
Inserting Images into a Presentation

Data Files

C:\091060Data\Adding Graphical Elements to Your Presentation\Develetech Ind.pptx

C:\091060Data\Adding Graphical Elements to Your Presentation\Videogame_Front.png

Scenario

You have completed your orientation and training at Develetech Industries, and you have begun working with one of the product development teams. Each team is developing one product that will be part of Develetech's next seasonal product roll out, New Visions Now. As part of the project kickoff, Develetech is holding a series of internal meetings to introduce the new products to Develetech employees. Members of the various design teams have begun putting together a PowerPoint presentation to introduce the new products. Your supervisor has asked you to add one more image of the video game console your team is developing, and to enhance the title slide.

1. Add an image to a slide using Bing Image Search.

   a) From the **C:\091060Data\Adding Graphical Elements to Your Presentation** folder, open the **Develetech Ind.pptx** file.
   b) In slide **1**, select **Insert→Images→Online Pictures**.
   c) In the **Insert Pictures** window, in the **Search Bing** text box, type *sun horizons* and then select the **Search** button.
   d) From the web search results, select an image of the sun on the horizon, and then select **Insert**.

2. Resize and align the image.

   a) Position the cursor at the top-right corner of the inserted image and then click and drag to resize the image so that it fits in the space below the "New Visions Now" text box.
   b) Position the cursor over the center of the image and when the pointer changes to cross-hairs, drag the image so that it is centered below the text.

3. Add an image to a slide from your computer.

   a) Navigate to slide **12**.

b) Select **Insert→Images→Pictures**.

c) In the **Insert Picture** dialog box, navigate to the **C:\091060Data\Adding Graphical Elements to Your Presentation** folder.

d) Select the **Videogame_Front.png** file, and then select **Insert**.

e) Drag the image so that it is positioned above the left-most image on the slide.

f) Click anywhere outside the image to deselect it.

4. Save the presentation to the **C:\091060Data\Adding Graphical Elements to Your Presentation** folder as *My Develetech Ind.pptx*

TOPIC B

Insert Shapes

Adding existing images to your presentations is a quick and effective way to illustrate key points to your audience. But you may not always have the right image for your message. You are likely to encounter situations in which it would be best to create your own graphics.

PowerPoint 2016 allows you to add and customize a variety of shapes to your presentations. Shapes can serve as visual cues, adding emphasis to other on-screen elements. You can also use shapes as text boxes, allowing you to create in-depth diagrams or flow charts, and giving you additional options for customizing your textual content.

Shapes

Shapes are common geometric objects that you can add to your PowerPoint presentations. PowerPoint 2016 contains a variety of pre-existing shapes that you can use to build complex figures or illustrations. You can also use shapes as text boxes, giving you further options for displaying text in your presentations. Like text boxes, shapes can also contain color, effects, and other style elements.

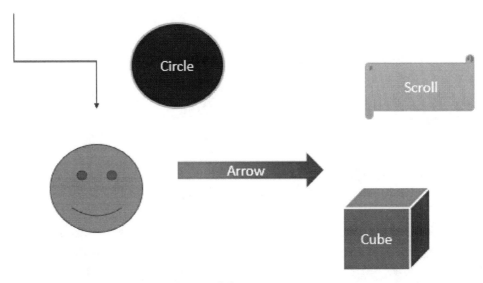

Figure 4–5: Shapes in a PowerPoint slide.

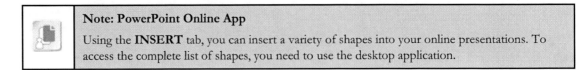

Note: PowerPoint Online App

Using the **INSERT** tab, you can insert a variety of shapes into your online presentations. To access the complete list of shapes, you need to use the desktop application.

The Drawing Tools Format Contextual Tab

PowerPoint 2016 provides you with a number of commands for modifying shapes in your presentation. You can access these commands on the **Drawing Tools Format** contextual tab whenever shapes or text boxes are selected.

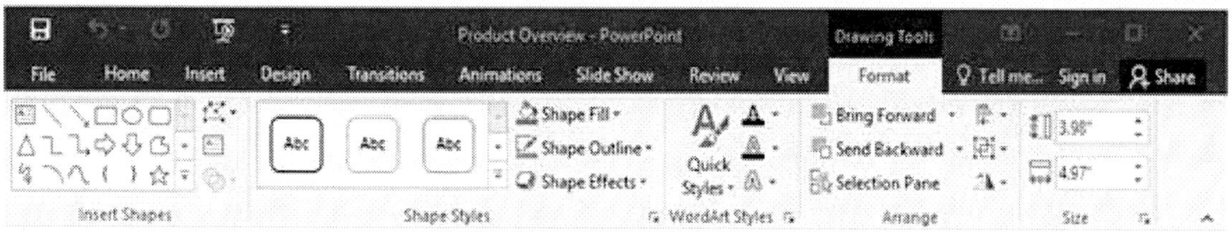

Figure 4-6: Commands on the Drawing Tools Format contextual tab.

The following table describes the **Drawing Tools Format** contextual tab commands.

Drawing Tools Format Contextual Tab Group	Contains Commands For
Insert Shapes	Inserting or modifying shapes in your presentation.
Shape Styles	Applying various style elements to shapes.
WordArt Styles	Applying various style elements to the text in your shapes.
Arrange	Arranging shapes and other objects on your slides.
Size	Adjusting the size of shapes and other objects on your slides.

> **Note:** The commands for modifying shapes are the same as the commands for modifying text boxes. Shapes are, essentially, a more complex version of text boxes.

> **Note: PowerPoint Online App**
>
> With the exception of the **WordArt Styles** and **Size** command groups, the **DRAWING TOOLS FORMAT** contextual tab provides these same commands in the online app as described here.

Shape Styles

Shape styles are quick styles that you can apply to a shape. They allow you to format shapes by using a combination of fills, effects, and outlines. The **Shape Styles** gallery includes several preset shape styles that you can apply to a shape. PowerPoint enables you to preview a shape style before applying it.

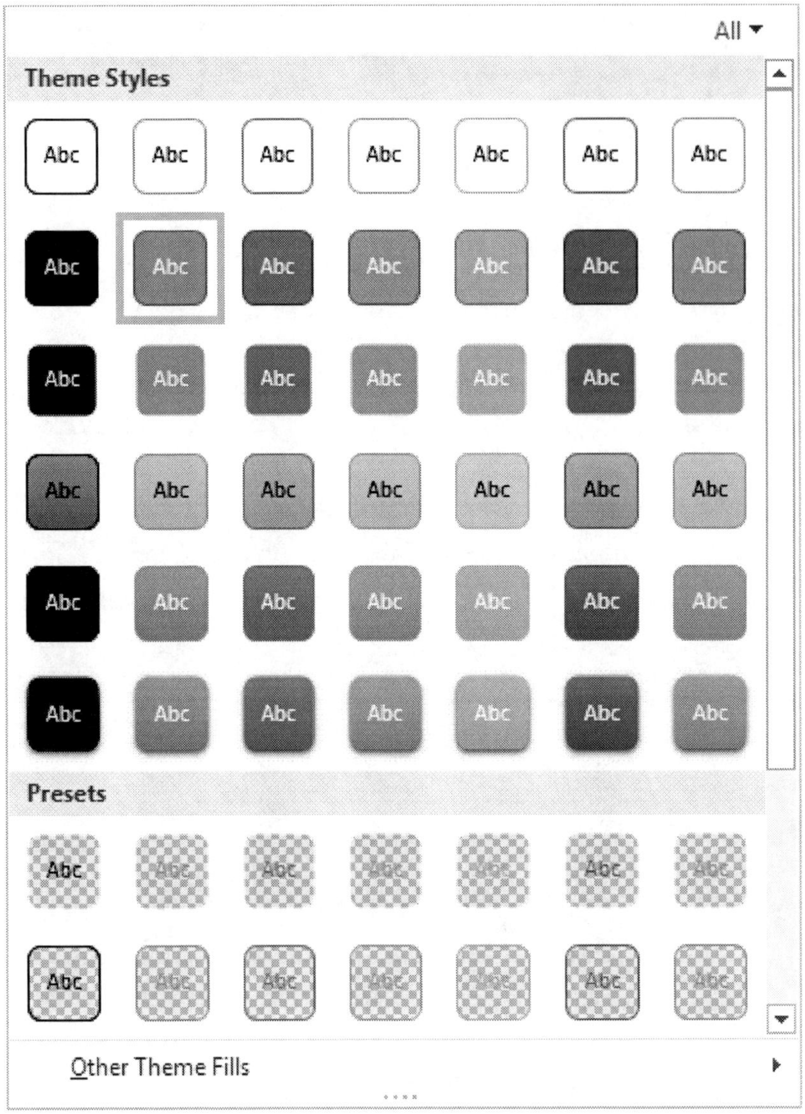

Figure 4–7: Preset styles available in the Shape Styles gallery.

> **Access the Checklist tile on your CHOICE Course screen for reference information and job aids on How to Insert Shapes.**

Custom Shapes

Sometimes, the default shapes available in PowerPoint will not suit your needs. When this happens, you can use the custom shape-creating features in PowerPoint 2016 to create new shapes. PowerPoint 2016 allows you to combine multiple shapes to create new, custom shapes, or to drag edit points on existing shapes to alter their appearance.

> **Note: PowerPoint Online App**
>
> This feature is not available in the online app; however, if you create custom shapes using PowerPoint 2016, they will be preserved and visible when the file is opened online.

The Merge Shapes Feature

The **Merge Shapes** feature provides you with options for combining two or more shapes on a slide into a new, custom shape. Once merged, the new shape typically displays as a single object, and all edits to the object will affect the entire shape. PowerPoint 2016 provides five options for merging shapes. These options determine the way the shapes are combined.

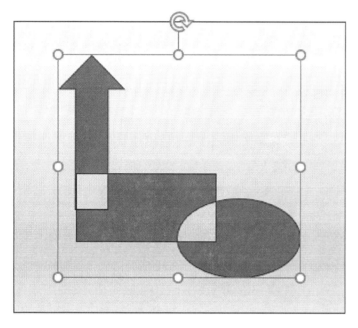

Figure 4–8: Several shapes combined into one on a PowerPoint slide.

The following table describes the options for combining shapes.

Merge Shapes Option	Combines Shapes Into
Union	A single solid shape. Any overlapped regions display as part of the new shape.
Combine	A single shape with the overlapped regions removed. The slide background will display through any removed regions.
Fragment	Multiple different shapes based on the overlapped regions of the original shapes. All areas of the original shapes that do not overlap, become new shapes. All overlapped regions also become new shapes. All shapes can be edited separately.
Intersect	A single shape defined by the region in which all selected shapes overlap each other.
Subtract	A single shape that is a variation of the first shape selected. The portions of the first shape selected that overlap with the other selected shapes are removed.

The Edit Points Tool

The **Edit Points** tool allows you to create new custom shapes by changing the outline of an existing shape. When you use the **Edit Points** tool, several edit points appear on the shape's outline allowing you to modify the shape. There are two types of edit points in PowerPoint 2016: black and white. The black edit points allow you to change the shape of the selected object, while the white edit points allow you to change the curvature of the line between two black edit points.

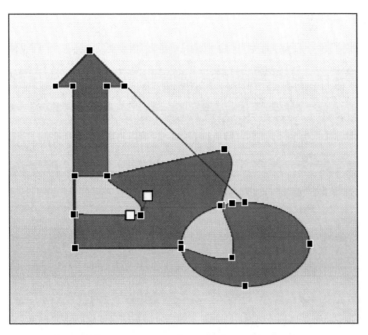

Figure 4-9: Edit points on a shape in PowerPoint.

Access the Checklist tile on your **CHOICE** Course screen for reference information and job aids on **How to Create Custom Shapes.**

ACTIVITY 4-2
Inserting Shapes

Before You Begin
The file My Develetech Ind.pptx is open.

Scenario
The new product images and several of the key slides are now in place for the new product presentation. Now, you will need to add product feature information about your team's design to the product slide. You decide to use shapes to display that information.

---

1. Add a shape to a slide.

   a) If necessary, on the **View** tab, in the **Show** group, check the **Rulers** check box.
   b) In slide **12**, select **Insert→Illustrations→Shapes**.
   c) From the **Shapes** gallery, in the **Rectangles** section, select **Rounded Rectangle**, which is the second option.
   d) At the top-right corner of the slide, click and drag the cursor to draw a rounded rectangle about 1/2 inch in height and 3 inches in width.

2. Add text to the shape.

   a) If necessary, select the shape you inserted.
   b) Type the text *Product Features* so that it appears within the rounded rectangle.
   c) Select **Home→Paragraph→Align Text→Top**.

   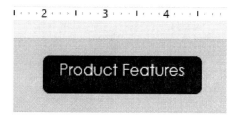

   d) If necessary, increase the size of the shape by dragging the resizing handle at the top-right corner so that the text appears in a single line within the shape.

3. Apply a shape style.

   a) On the **Drawing Tools** contextual tab, on the **Format** tab, in the **Shape Styles** group, select the **More** button.
   b) From the **Shape Styles** gallery, in the **Presets** section, select the **Semitransparent - Dark Blue, Accent 1, No Outline** style, which is the second item in the third row.

4. Apply a pattern fill to the shape.

   a) In the **Shape Styles** group, select the dialog box launcher to display the **Format Shape** pane.
   b) If necessary, select the **Shape Options** section, and ensure that the **Fill & Line** tab ◇ is selected.
   c) Expand the **Fill** section, and then select the **Pattern fill** option.
   d) From the **Pattern** gallery, select the **70%** pattern ▉, which is the third item in the second row.

---

5. Apply effects to the shape.

   a) Select the **Effects** tab  and then expand the **Glow** section.

   b) Select the **Presets** button.

   c) From the **Glow Variations** gallery, select **Dark Blue, 18 pt glow, Accent color 1** which is the first item in the last row.

   d) Select the **Color** button.

   e) In the **Theme Colors** menu, select **Dark Blue, Background 2** which is the third item in the top row.

   f) Close the **Format Shape** pane.

6. Set the shape formatting as the default shape formatting for the presentation.

   a) If necessary, select the shape.

   b) Right-click and select **Set as Default Shape**.

   c) Navigate to slide **10**.

   d) Select **Insert→Illustrations→Shapes**.

   e) From the **Shapes** gallery, in the **Rectangles** section, select **Rectangle**, which is the first item.

   f) At the top-right corner of the slide, click and drag the cursor to draw a rectangle about 1/2 inches in height and 3 inches in width.

7. Create a custom shape.

   a) Select **Insert→Illustrations→Shapes**.

   b) From the **Shapes** gallery, in the **Rectangles** section, select **Rounded Rectangle**.

   c) At a few inches within the bottom-left corner of the rectangle, click and drag the cursor to draw a rounded rectangle about 6 inches in height and 3 inches in width.

 Note: A small portion of the rounded rectangle should overlap with the rectangle.

   d) Hold down **Shift** and select the rectangle.

   e) On the **Drawing Tools** contextual tab, select **Format→Insert Shapes→Merge Shapes→Union**.

f) Type the text *Laptop Models* within the shape.

g) Save and close the file.

Summary

In this lesson, you inserted images and shapes into a presentation. Your presentation has come a long way since you first created and saved it. You have a dynamic, well-organized presentation with text, images, and graphics. You are now familiar with how to add a variety of multimedia elements to your presentation.

Which of the embedded graphical content functions do you think will be the most useful as you create presentations in PowerPoint?

What are some creative and effective ways that you have seen people use graphics in PowerPoint presentations? What kind of impact did they have on you as an audience member?

Note: Check your CHOICE Course screen for opportunities to interact with your classmates, peers, and the larger CHOICE online community about the topics covered in this course or other topics you are interested in. From the Course screen you can also access available resources for a more continuous learning experience.

5 | Modifying Objects in Your Presentation

Lesson Time: 1 hour, 15 minutes

Lesson Introduction

Adding a variety of elements to your presentation is a powerful way to deliver your message and keep your audience interested. But showing too many objects on screen all at once, or objects that don't seem to fit well together, can clutter the screen and distract the audience. When you work with a larger variety of multimedia objects, you run the risk of putting too much content on your slides.

The ability to modify and arrange on-screen objects can help you avoid clutter and create slides with a sense of balance and continuity. By utilizing the graphical editing capabilities in Microsoft® Office PowerPoint® 2016, you can avoid the pitfalls of slide clutter and deliver a well-balanced, aesthetically pleasing presentation.

Lesson Objectives

In this lesson, you will:

- Edit objects.

- Format objects.

- Group objects.

- Arrange objects.

- Animate objects.

TOPIC A

Edit Objects

Sometimes, objects just don't mesh well together on screen. There might be too much content on a slide. If an image is too big, text may look out of place next to it. Or, you may inadvertently give an object too much emphasis when it is not the focus of your message. You can make simple changes to on-screen objects to fix these problems.

As you include more and more graphical content, you are most likely to end up having to make some adjustments to keep your presentation fresh and pleasing to the eye. PowerPoint has a number of editing features that allow you to tailor your graphics to suit your needs.

Object Selection Methods

To modify an object on a slide, you must first select it. Once you select an object, it becomes active and will be displayed with the border, sizing handles, and rotation handle. PowerPoint 2016 provides you with a number of methods for selecting a single object or multiple objects, such as selecting the on-screen objects, using keyboard shortcuts, using the **Select** drop-down menu, and using the **Selection Pane**.

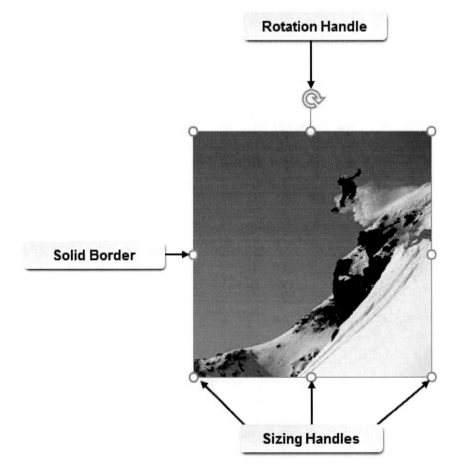

Figure 5-1: An image in the selected state.

Note: PowerPoint Online App

You can select objects in the online app by using the mouse or keyboard shortcuts; however, the **Select** button on the **HOME** tab and the **Selection** pane are not available.

Access the Checklist tile on your CHOICE Course screen for reference information and job aids on How to Select Objects.

The Crop Tool

You may want to add an image to your presentation that contains some content that you don't want to display. *Cropping* an image allows you to include only the parts of the image that you want. Think of cropping as being similar to cutting a physical photograph with a pair of scissors. The **Crop** tool in PowerPoint enables you to crop unwanted portions from an image.

Figure 5-2: An image before and after cropping in PowerPoint.

Note: PowerPoint Online App

You can crop images in the online app; however, the available **Crop** tool is a straightforward crop with no advanced features, such as cropping to a shape.

The Picture Tools Format Contextual Tab

It may be necessary to make corrections or adjustments to the images in your presentation. The **Picture Tools Format** contextual tab provides you with access to PowerPoint's array of picture formatting and correction tools. The table lists the groups in the **Picture Tools Format** contextual tab and identifies the options available in them.

Figure 5-3: The options in the Picture Tools Format contextual tab.

The following table describes the **Picture Tools Format** contextual tab options.

Picture Tools Group	Provides Commands To
Adjust	Adjust the color, contrast, and brightness of images, and to remove image backgrounds.
Picture Styles	Format an image's shape, border, or outline, and apply image effects.
Arrange	Position images on slides.
Size	Resize, crop, and rotate images.

Note: PowerPoint Online App

The **PICTURE TOOLS FORMAT** tab provides commands to make basic changes to the pictures, such as applying a picture style, changing the arrangement, rotating, or cropping the picture.

The Format Picture Pane

The **Format Picture** pane provides you with a variety of commands you can use to format the images that you add to a presentation. While many of the commands available in the **Format Picture** pane are similar to those found in the **Format Shape** pane, there are some differences. For example, the **Format Picture** pane is not divided into **Shape Options** and **Text Options** sections like the **Format Shape** pane. These commands are not necessary for images because the images themselves can't contain PowerPoint-generated text.

Note: You can place a text box with no fill over an image to create the illusion of text in the image.

Additionally, within the **Size & Properties** tab in the **Format Picture** pane, the commands in the **Text Box** section are grayed out. Again, these commands are not necessary for formatting an image, like they are for text boxes, shapes, and some other objects.

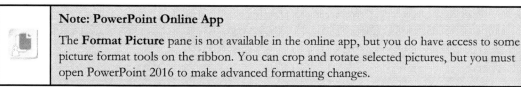

Figure 5-4: Options in the Format Picture pane.

Fill Options

You can apply fills and other background formatting to images in PowerPoint 2016. However, these will appear only if you have cropped part of the image or applied transparency to some portion of the image.

> **Note: PowerPoint Online App**
>
> The **Format Picture** pane is not available in the online app, but you do have access to some picture format tools on the ribbon. You can crop and rotate selected pictures, but you must open PowerPoint 2016 to make advanced formatting changes.

The Remove Background Tool

The *Remove Background tool* allows you to remove background elements from images, leaving only the subject elements that you would like to include from the image. This tool can automatically determine what is in the background and what is the main subject of the image. It also provides you with commands that you can use to select which elements of an image to keep and which to remove.

> **Note:** You cannot use the **Remove Background** tool for vector graphic files, such as Scalable Vector Graphics (SVG), Adobe® Illustrator® Graphics (AI), Windows® Metafile Format (WMF), and Vector Drawing (DRW).

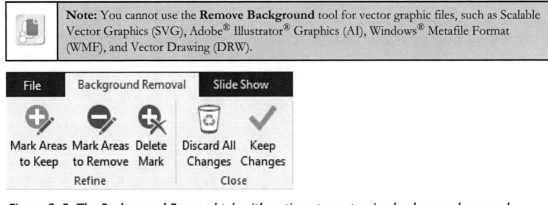

Figure 5-5: The Background Removal tab with options to customize background removal settings.

The following table describes the **Background Removal** tab options.

Background Removal Tab Option	Function
Mark Areas to Keep	Enables you to draw lines to mark areas to keep in the picture.
Mark Areas to Remove	Enables you to draw lines to mark areas to remove from the picture.
Delete Mark	Deletes any lines you have drawn either to keep or remove areas of the picture.
Discard All Changes	Closes the **Background Removal** tab without making any changes to the original picture.
Keep Changes	Removes the background, either automatically or according to the lines you have drawn, and closes the **Background Removal** tab.

> **Note: PowerPoint Online App**
>
> This feature is not available in the online app. If you need to remove the background from a picture, you must use the desktop application.

The Object Resizing Methods

Resizing is the process of changing the height and width of an object. You can use the sizing handles to resize a selected object, or you can use the commands in the ribbon to adjust the height and width of the object.

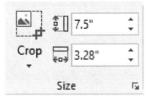

Figure 5-6: Resizing options in the ribbon.

> **Note: PowerPoint Online App**
>
> As previously mentioned, you can crop an image in the online app; however, the other Size group commands are only available in the desktop application.

The Object Scaling Methods

Scaling an object is similar to resizing an object. However, with scaling, you maintain the original ratio of height to width of the object. PowerPoint 2016 provides you with several scaling options on the **Format Picture** pane.

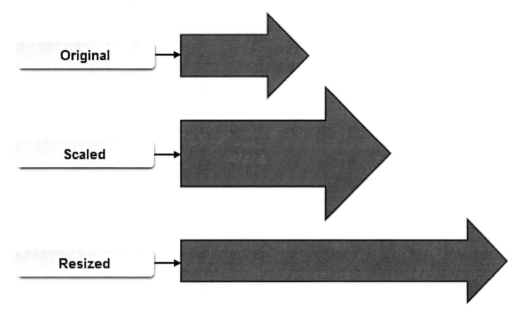

Figure 5-7: Effects of scaling versus resizing an object.

The following table describes the object scaling options.

Scaling Option	Description
Lock aspect ratio	Automatically adjusts the height of an object as you adjust its width, and vice versa. This ensures true scaling.
Relative to original picture size	If you have altered an image's original aspect ratio, this feature will restore the original aspect ratio upon further size adjustments.
Best scale for slide show	Prevents objects such as bitmaps and some movie clips from appearing distorted when presenting a slide show.

Note: The scaling options you specified are applicable only when using the commands in the **Format Picture** pane or on the ribbon. If you resize an object with the diagonal resizing handles, it always scales. If you resize it by using the top, bottom, or side resizing handles, scale is not preserved.

Note: PowerPoint Online App

This feature is not available in the online app. If you need to modify the scale of an image, you must use the desktop application.

The Object Orientation Options

Orientation refers to the angle at which you display the objects on your slides. PowerPoint gives you the ability to rotate objects at any angle and flip objects horizontally and vertically. When an object is selected, you can rotate it either clockwise or counterclockwise using the rotation handle. There are also several orientation options that you can apply to objects.

Orientation Option	Allows You To
Rotate Right 90°	Rotate an object one quarter turn to the right.
Rotate Left 90°	Rotate an object one quarter turn to the left.
Flip Vertical	Flip an object across the vertical plane. This is not the same as rotating an object 180 degrees. This option creates a vertical mirror image of the object.
Flip Horizontal	Flip an object across the horizontal plane to create a mirror image of the original object.
More Rotation Options	Access the **Size & Properties** tab in the **Format Picture** pane. Using the options on the tab, you can rotate an object in one-degree increments.

Note: PowerPoint Online App

You can rotate images in the online app; however, the available orientation options are limited to **Flip Vertical** and **Flip Horizontal**.

The Image Compression Options

Adding a large number of images to your presentation will, naturally, make your presentation's file size large. *Image compression* allows you to reduce the file size of the images in your presentation, reducing the overall size of the presentation file. This can aid the process of storing or sharing your presentation. You can access image compression options through the **Compress Pictures** dialog box.

Compress Pictures   ?   X

Compression options:

☑ Apply only to this picture
☑ Delete cropped areas of pictures

Target output:

○ HD (330 ppi): good quality for high-definition (HD) displays
○ Print (220 ppi): excellent quality on most printers and screens
○ Web (150 ppi): good for web pages and projectors
○ E-mail (96 ppi): minimize document size for sharing
● Use document resolution

OK   Cancel

Figure 5–8: Image compression options in the Compress Pictures dialog box.

The following table describes the compression options.

Compression Option	Description
Apply only to this picture	When checked, this option applies compression to only the selected image.
Delete cropped areas of pictures	When checked, this option instructs PowerPoint to delete any part of an image that has been cropped out before compressing images. This further reduces the overall file size.

Compression Option	Description
HD (330 ppi)	Target output resolution for images that is ideal for High-Definition (HD) displays.
Print (220 ppi)	Target output resolution for images that is ideal for most printers and screens.
Web (150 ppi)	Target output resolution for images that is good for web pages and projectors.
E-mail (96 ppi)	Target output resolution for images that is ideal for document sharing.
Use document resolution	This option uses the document resolution setting that a user has defined in the project options for a PowerPoint presentation.

Note: Target output options will be grayed out in the **Compress Pictures** dialog box if the resolution of the original image is less than the particular option. In other words, you cannot increase the resolution of an image.

Note: PowerPoint Online App

This feature is not available in the online app. If you need to compress an image, you must use the desktop application.

Access the Checklist tile on your CHOICE Course screen for reference information and job aids on How to Edit Objects in Your Presentation.

ACTIVITY 5-1
Editing Objects in Your Presentation

Data Files

C:\091060Data\Modifying Objects in Your Presentation\Develetech Ind_Objects.pptx

C:\091060Data\Modifying Objects in Your Presentation\New Sunset.JPG

Scenario

After reviewing the presentation, you and several other members of your team decide that some of the graphics don't quite suit the project. You decide to change the image on the title slide, and remove the background of the image used on a section header slide.

1. Replace the image on the title slide with another image.
   a) From the **C:\091060Data\Modifying Objects in Your Presentation** folder, open the **Develetech Ind_Objects.pptx** file.
   b) In slide **1**, select the image below the "New Visions Now" text.
   c) On the **Picture Tools** contextual tab, select **Format→Adjust→Change Picture**.
   d) In the **Insert Pictures** window, in the **From a file** section, select **Browse**.
   e) In the **Insert Picture** dialog box, navigate to the **C:\091060Data\Modifying Objects in Your Presentation** folder.
   f) Select the **New Sunset.JPG** file, and then select **Insert**.

2. Crop the image.
   a) On the **Picture Tools** contextual tab, select **Format→Size→Crop**.
   b) Drag the top cropping handle downwards to crop out the tree at the top of the image.
   c) Select **Format→Size→Crop** to remove the cropped out portions from the image.

3. Scale the image to fit the screen.
   a) Ensure that the image is still selected.
   b) On the **Format** tab, in the **Size** group, select the dialog box launcher to display the **Format Picture** pane.
   c) On the **Size & Properties** tab 🔳, in the **Size** section, ensure that the **Lock aspect ratio** check box is checked.
   d) In the **Scale Height** field, select the up-arrow button of the spin box several times to increase the height to 100%.
   e) Close the **Format Picture** pane.
   f) Drag the image so that it is centered below the "New Visions Now" text.

4. Add an effect to the image.
   a) Select **Format→Adjust→Artistic Effects**.
   b) From the gallery, select **Texturizer**, which is the second tile in the fourth row.

5. Apply a color correction to the image.
   a) Select **Format→Adjust→Corrections**.

b) From the gallery, in the **Brightness/Contrast** category, select **Brightness: 0% (Normal) Contrast: +20%,** which is the third tile in the fourth row.

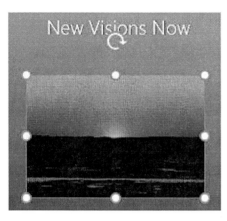

6. Remove the background from an image.

a) Navigate to slide **4** and select the image.

b) Select **Format→Adjust→Remove Background**.

c) On the rectangle above the image, drag the resizing handle on the right up to the right border of the image.

 Note: By resizing the rectangle, you can ensure that the required portions of the image are not marked for removal.

d) Similarly, drag the resizing handle at the bottom of the rectangle up to the bottom border of the image.

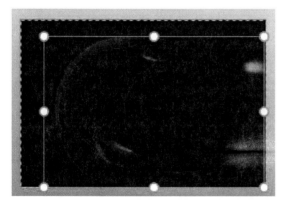

e) On the **Background Removal** tab, in the **Close** group, select **Keep Changes**.

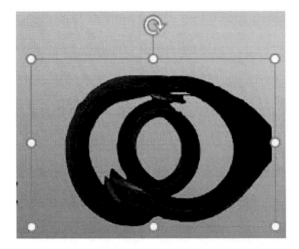

7. Save the file in the **C:\091060Data\Modifying Objects in Your Presentation** folder as *My Develetech Ind_Objects.pptx*

TOPIC B

Format Objects

You have modified the objects in your presentation. They are now the right size, the correct color, and have the artistic effects you prefer. But they still might not seem quite right. Some images may not be a good fit for themes that you have applied to the presentation. Other images may still look cluttered when viewed next to text, even though they are well proportioned on the slide.

It is often necessary to add formatting to the objects in your presentation to further help offset them from other on-screen elements, and help them fit in with the overall look of your project. By adding object formatting, you will refine your presentation for clarity, and ensure your visual content meshes well with your textual content and overall presentation theme. And here's the good news: formatting objects in your presentations is very much the same as formatting text boxes and shapes, which you have already done.

The Picture Formatting Options

The **Picture Styles** gallery provides you with access to a variety of pre-configured formatting styles for pictures that you add to your presentations. The picture formatting options include many of the formatting options available for all objects, as well as formatting specific to pictures, such as adding picture frames.

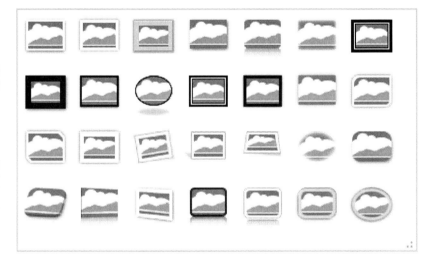

Figure 5-9: The Picture Styles gallery with formatting configurations that are specific to pictures.

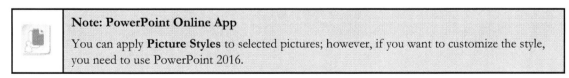

Note: PowerPoint Online App

You can apply **Picture Styles** to selected pictures; however, if you want to customize the style, you need to use PowerPoint 2016.

The Set Transparent Color Option

The **Set Transparent Color** option allows you to make one of the colors present in an image transparent. When this option is applied, it sets all the pixels of the selected color transparent throughout the image.

 Access the Checklist tile on your CHOICE Course screen for reference information and job aids on How to Format Pictures and Objects.

ACTIVITY 5-2
Formatting Pictures and Objects

Before You Begin

The file My Develetech Ind_Objects.pptx is open.

Scenario

You have finished editing the objects in the presentation. You and others on the team feel some of the on-screen objects don't stand out from the background as well as they should. You also think the pattern background in the shapes makes the text difficult to read. You decide to add some formatting to the objects in the presentation to help them stand out and to improve readability.

---

1. **Format the image border.**

   a) Navigate to slide **1** and select the image.

   b) On the **Picture Tools** contextual tab, select **Format→Picture Styles→Picture Border** down arrow.

   c) From the **Theme Colors** gallery, select **Dark Blue, Background 2**, which is the third tile in the first row.

   d) Select **Format→Picture Styles→Picture Border** down arrow, and then select **Weight→3 pt**.

2. **Apply a shadow effect to the image.**

   a) Select **Format→Picture Styles→Picture Effects→Shadow→Shadow Options**.

   b) In the **Format Picture** pane, ensure that the **Effects** tab ⬠ is selected, and the **Shadow** section is displayed.

   c) Select the **Presets** button.

   d) In the gallery, in the **Outer** section, select **Offset Diagonal Bottom Right**, which is the first tile in the first row.

   e) In the **Transparency** field, drag the slider to the left to set the transparency to **10%**.

   f) In the **Size** field, select the up-arrow button on the spin box to increase the shadow size to **101%**.

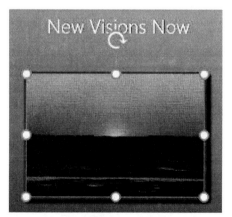

   g) Close the **Format Picture** pane.

3. **Format a shape.**

   a) Navigate to slide **5** and select the rounded rectangle shape with the text "Product Features."

---

b) On the **Drawing Tools** contextual tab, on the **Format** tab, in the **Shape Styles** group, select the **More** button.

c) From the **Shape Styles** gallery, in the **Theme Styles** section, select **Light 1 Outline, Colored Fill - Dark Blue, Accent 1**, which is the second tile in the third row.

4. Save the changes to the file.

TOPIC C

Group Objects

Knowing how to add objects to your presentations, and how to format those objects, gives you the ability to create and deliver a presentation that will wow your audience. However, the task of individually formatting all of these objects can be daunting and time consuming. So, how do you make your presentation sparkle while staying on schedule?

PowerPoint 2016 gives you the ability to link together multiple objects within a presentation to make modifying them quick and easy. In addition to saving you time and effort, this can also help you maintain a consistent look to your graphical content throughout your presentation.

> **Note: PowerPoint Online App**
> The Grouping feature is not available in the online app. If you want to use this feature, you must use PowerPoint 2016.

The Grouping Feature

The *Grouping feature* allows you to link multiple objects on one slide together, effectively making them a single object. When you apply formatting to the group, it will apply to all of the objects within the group. When you select grouped items, they all display within a single border, with sizing handles and a rotation handle for the entire group.

You can still resize, rotate, and apply formatting to individual objects within a group. When a group is selected, you can select an individual object you would like to format independently. The object will appear with its own border and sizing handles, indicating that you can resize or format it without affecting the rest of the group.

Figure 5-10: Objects grouped together on a PowerPoint slide.

> **Access the Checklist tile on your CHOICE Course screen for reference information and job aids on How to Group and Ungroup Objects.**

ACTIVITY 5-3
Grouping Objects

Before You Begin

The My Develetech Ind_Objects.pptx file is open.

Scenario

You notice that the product images in the presentation appear a bit smaller compared to the shapes, and you feel they look a bit flat on screen. You decide to resize the images in one of the slides and apply a 3-D Rotation effect to improve the overall look of the slide. You realize grouping the images before modifying them will save you time and give you consistent results for all of the objects on the slide.

1. Group the objects on a slide.
   a) If necessary, navigate to slide **5**.
   b) Select the image of the tablet PC at the top of the slide, and then hold down **Shift** and select the other two product images.
   c) On the **Picture Tools** contextual tab, select **Format→Arrange→Group→Group**.

2. Resize the group.
   a) Ensure that the group is selected and that all three images are displayed within a single border.
   b) If necessary, on the **Picture Tools** contextual tab, select the **Format** tab.
   c) In the **Size** group, select the dialog box launcher to display the **Format Picture** pane.
   d) On the **Size & Properties** tab, in the **Size** section, check the **Lock aspect ratio** check box.
   e) In the **Scale Width** field, select the up arrow button on the spin box several times to increase the width to **115%**.
   f) Close the **Format Picture** pane.

3. Apply a 3-D rotation effect to the group.
   a) Select **Format→Picture Styles→Picture Effects→3-D Rotation**.

b) From the **3-D Rotation** gallery, in the **Perspective** section, select **Perspective Above**, which is the first tile in the second row.

4. Save the changes to the file.

TOPIC D

Arrange Objects

You have put a lot of effort toward adding visually appealing graphical content, and editing and formatting it. Your presentation has a professional look and is already well-polished. You can't help but feel, though, that some of the graphics and images look cluttered or chaotic. And some of the more important visual elements of your slides are getting lost among the others. So, what do you do?

PowerPoint provides you with a number of options for arranging the objects in your presentation that can help you create a sense of balance, and distinguish some objects from others. These options can also help you add depth to your slides, enhance the visual appeal of your presentation, and emphasize key graphics.

Object Order

Object order defines how objects that overlap appear on your slides in relation to each other. An object on the front layer will appear fully visible, regardless of whether or not it overlaps with other objects. An object on the back layer will be partially or completely hidden behind objects that overlap it. PowerPoint provides several object order commands that you can use to layer objects on your slides. Using these commands helps to avoid clutter and assign a level of importance to certain objects over others.

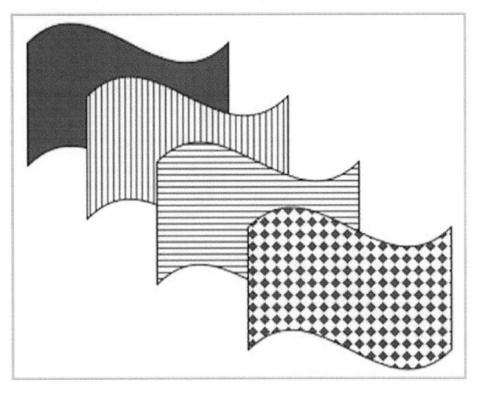

Figure 5-11: Objects on different layers in a PowerPoint slide.

Object Order Option	Moves the Selected Object
Bring Forward	Forward so that it is hidden by fewer objects.

Object Order Option	Moves the Selected Object
Bring to Front	In front of all other objects so that no part of it is hidden behind another object.
Send Backward	Back so that it is hidden by the objects that are in front of it.
Send to Back	Behind all other objects.

Guides and Gridlines

Guides are lines that allow you to accurately position objects on a slide. The default guides in PowerPoint 2016 appear as a single horizontal line and a single vertical line that intersect at the center of the slides in a presentation. You can add and reposition guides on your slides to suit your needs.

Gridlines display as multiple horizontal and vertical dotted lines, forming a grid on the slides in a presentation. Like guides, gridlines can help you accurately place objects on your slides. Unlike guides, you cannot add or remove gridlines, but you can adjust the spacing between them to suit your needs.

Figure 5-12: Guides and gridlines on a PowerPoint slide.

> **Note: PowerPoint Online App**
>
> This feature is not available in the online app; however, you can use guides and gridlines in PowerPoint 2016.

> Access the Checklist tile on your **CHOICE Course** screen for reference information and job aids on **How to Arrange and Align Objects**.

ACTIVITY 5-4
Arranging Objects

Before You Begin

The My Develetech Ind_Objects.pptx file is open.

Scenario

You have inserted a slide introducing the new Develetech product names, but your supervisor doesn't like the layout of the shapes on the slide. She has asked you to create a more layered look to the shapes. You decide to arrange and align the shapes on the slide to appear layered.

1. Make the guides and gridlines visible.

   a) Navigate to slide **3**.
   b) On the **View** tab, in the **Show** group, check the **Guides** check box.
   c) On the **View** tab, in the **Show** group, check the **Gridlines** check box.

2. Use the guides and the gridlines to align the shapes.

   a) Select the shape with the text "Knomatico," and then hold down **Shift** and select the shapes with the text "GeoExis" and "Handia."
   b) On the **Home** tab, in the **Drawing** group, select the dialog box launcher to display the **Format Shape** pane.
   c) Select the **Size & Properties** tab and then expand the **Position** section.
   d) In the **Horizontal position** spin box, select the up arrow button several times until the right edge of the selected shapes aligns with the vertical guide.
   e) Select the two shapes with the text "Melius" and "Protoi."

f) In the **Format Shape** pane, in the **Horizontal position** text box, replace the existing value with *4.2* and press **Enter**.

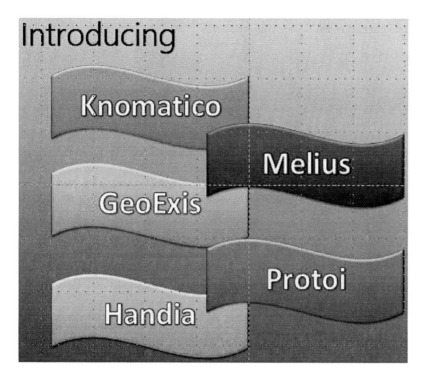

g) Close the **Format Shape** pane.
h) On the **View** tab, in the **Show** group, uncheck the **Gridlines** and the **Guides** check boxes.

3. Arrange the shapes on the slide.

a) Select the shape with the text "Knomatico."
b) On the **Drawing Tools** contextual tab, select **Format→Arrange→Bring Forward** down arrow, and then select **Bring to Front**.
c) Select the shape with the text "Protoi."
d) Select **Format→Arrange→Send Backward** down arrow, and then select **Send Backward**.
e) Repeat the previous step until the shape with the text "Protoi "is moved behind the shape with the text "GeoExis."
f) Select the shape with the text "Handia."
g) Select **Format→Arrange→Send Backward** down arrow, and then select **Send to Back**.

h) Click outside the shape to deselect it.

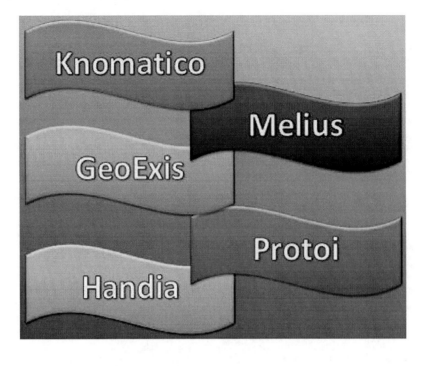

4. Save the changes to the file.

TOPIC E

Animate Objects

Graphics and images can make your presentation look professional, clarify your key points, and add visual appeal for your audience. But too many static images in sequence appearing within a short period of time can make your presentation look monotonous. The pictures and shapes that you have so carefully formatted could end up boring the audience, distracting their attention from your message.

Now that you have your fully formatted visuals in place, you will want to consider adding animation to keep your presentation interesting. PowerPoint 2016 gives you the ability to create and customize animation effects that can enhance your presentation and help you further emphasize key points.

Built-In Animation Effects

PowerPoint 2016 contains a wide variety of built-in animation effects that can transform your static graphics and text into engaging animations. You can apply animation effects to multiple objects on the same slide or to a single object. Animations can help you emphasize particular graphical elements, grab the audience's attention, and, perhaps, add a bit of humor when appropriate. PowerPoint also provides you with many options for modifying effects. For example, you can change the direction that an object moves or rotates.

Figure 5-13: The options to apply animations.

Animations are divided into four main categories, with a variety of specific effects in each category.

Animation Category	Use These To
Entrance	Move objects into frame or fade them in.
Emphasis	Draw the audience's attention to a particular object.
Exit	Move objects out of frame or fade them out.
Motion Paths	Generate on-screen motion for particular objects.

> **Note: PowerPoint Online App**
>
> There is a limited number of available animations and formatting options in the online app; however, all animations that are applied in PowerPoint 2016 will be preserved when you run the slideshow online.

> **Note:** To further explore animations, you can access the LearnTO **Effectively Use PowerPoint Animations and Transitions** presentation from the **LearnTO** tile on the CHOICE Course screen.

The Animation Painter Tool

The *Animation Painter tool* allows you to reapply animation effects to multiple objects. This feature works much like the **Format Painter** tool does for text formatting, only for animation. The sticky mode of the **Animation Painter** tool allows you to apply the same animation effect to multiple objects within your presentation, and in other presentations.

 Access the Checklist tile on your CHOICE Course screen for reference information and job aids on How to Animate Objects.

ACTIVITY 5-5
Animating Objects

Before You Begin
The My Develetech Ind_Objects.pptx file is open.

Scenario
You are pleased with the new alignment and the new arrangement of the shapes in your presentation. However, because the new product line announcement is such a big event, you feel the slide that lists the product names should be more exciting. You decide to use animation to add energy to the slide.

1. Apply an animation effect to a shape.

    a) In slide 3, select the shape with the text "Knomatico."

    b) On the **Animations** tab, in the **Animation** group, select the **More** button.

    c) From the **Animation** gallery, in the **Entrance** section, select **Grow & Turn**.

    d) Ensure that the shape with the text "Knomatico" is selected and then select **Animations→Animation→Effect Options→By Paragraph**.

2. Use the **Animation Painter** tool.

    a) Select the shape with the text "Knomatico," and then select **Animations→Advanced Animation→Animation Painter**.

    b) Select the shape with the text "Melius."

3. Use sticky mode to apply the animation to multiple shapes.

    a) Ensure that the shape with the text "Melius" is selected, and on the **Animations** tab, in the **Advanced Animation** group, double-click **Animation Painter**.

    b) Select the shapes with the text "GeoExis," "Protoi," and "Handia" one after the other to apply the animation effect to each.

    > **Note:** You may have to select the shapes once to activate them, and then select them again to apply the animation.

    c) Select **Animations→Advanced Animation→Animation Painter**.

    d) Click anywhere outside the shape with the text "Handia" to deselect it.

    e) Select **Animations→Preview→Preview**.

4. Save the changes and close the file.

Summary

In this lesson, you created a true multimedia presentation, complete with succinct text, engaging graphics, and dynamic animations. Your audience is sure to appreciate and enjoy the presentation. More importantly, the audience will be able pick out and focus on the important points within your message as you have prominently placed and emphasized them on your slides.

Which of the object-formatting options available in PowerPoint 2016 do you think will save you the most time while helping you create high-impact presentations?

In your experience, how might the addition of animations to presentation graphics enhance the overall experience of viewing the presentation? Are there situations in which animations would not be appropriate?

 Note: Check your CHOICE Course screen for opportunities to interact with your classmates, peers, and the larger CHOICE online community about the topics covered in this course or other topics you are interested in. From the Course screen you can also access available resources for a more continuous learning experience.

6 | Adding Tables to Your Presentation

Lesson Time: 20 minutes

Lesson Introduction

People commonly use Microsoft® Office PowerPoint® 2016 to create presentations for work meetings and other business-related purposes. It is likely that you will give a presentation that will contain sales figures, budgetary information, or other financial data. Or, perhaps you will need to give a presentation containing scientific data related to a study. When tasked with presenting financial information and other data in a presentation, you will need a way to display the information to the audience without endless slides of figure-dense content.

PowerPoint 2016 gives you the ability to easily add, populate, and work with tables in your presentations. Using tables is an effective way to convey large volumes of numerical content to your audience in an easy-to-digest format.

Lesson Objectives

In this lesson, you will:

- Create a table.

- Format a table.

- Insert a table from other Microsoft applications.

TOPIC A

Create a Table

Your presentation is nearly complete, and you are happy with the progress you have made. You have honed your message, and your text, graphics, and animations are all in place. You are confident that you can deliver a high-impact, engaging presentation to the audience. Now, you need to include financial and statistical data to your presentation to support your key points.

Numerical data is difficult to present to an audience through text and images alone. Without organizing such data into an easily read or easily interpreted format, your audience will likely miss key information and become frustrated trying to follow the presentation. Using the table features in PowerPoint 2016 can help you present data to your audience in a clear, concise manner.

Tables

Tables are containers for numerical data and other content that are organized into columns and rows of individual *cells*. Tables can range from simple objects with just a few cells, to large, complex objects that contain massive amounts of content. You can format tables with a variety of borders, effects, and styles.

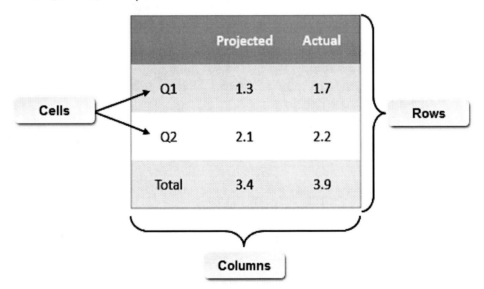

Figure 6-1: A table in PowerPoint.

> **Note: PowerPoint Online App**
>
> When using the online app, the only way to insert a table is to select **INSERT→Tables→Table** and then select the desired number of columns and rows. The other methods are only available in PowerPoint 2016.

Table Creation Options

PowerPoint 2016 provides you with several options for creating tables in your presentation. You can create a table by graphically selecting the desired number of columns and rows from the **Insert Table** drop-down menu. You can numerically select the number of columns and rows by using the **Insert Table** dialog box. PowerPoint 2016 also enables you to draw a custom table.

> **Note:** You can use smart guides to align the tables in your slides. In PowerPoint 2016, smart guides are not turned off when you create a table.

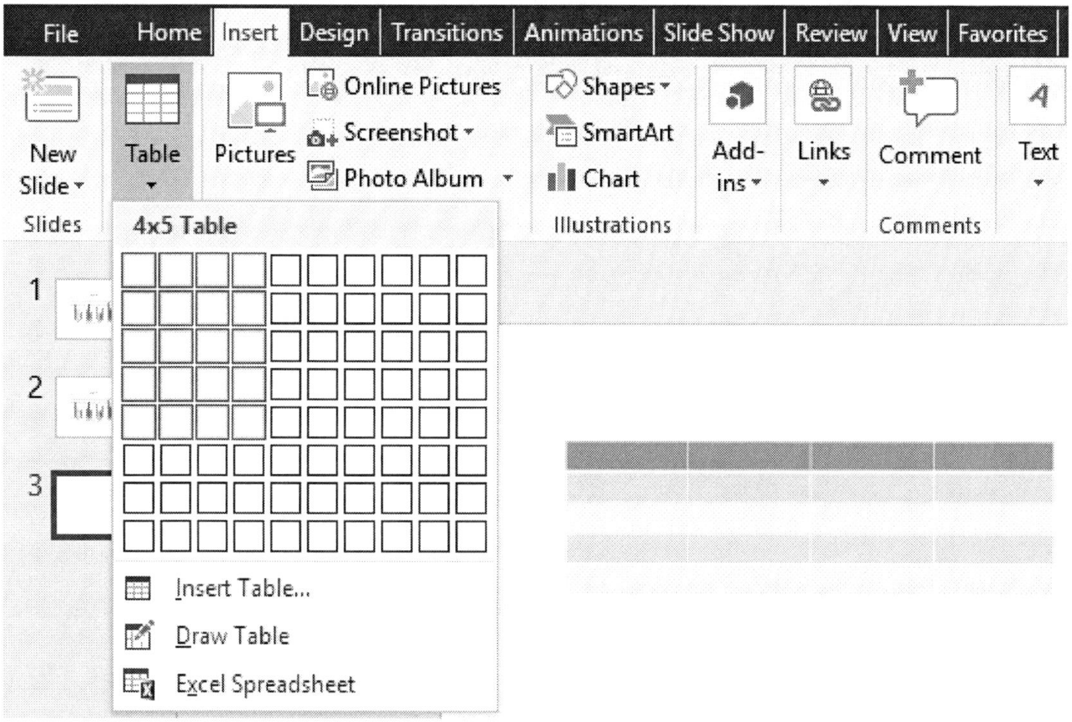

Figure 6-2: Table creation with the Insert Table drop-down menu.

The Insert Table Dialog Box

The **Insert Table** dialog box enables you to create tables by specifying the number of rows and columns you desire. If required, you can add more rows and columns after the table is inserted.

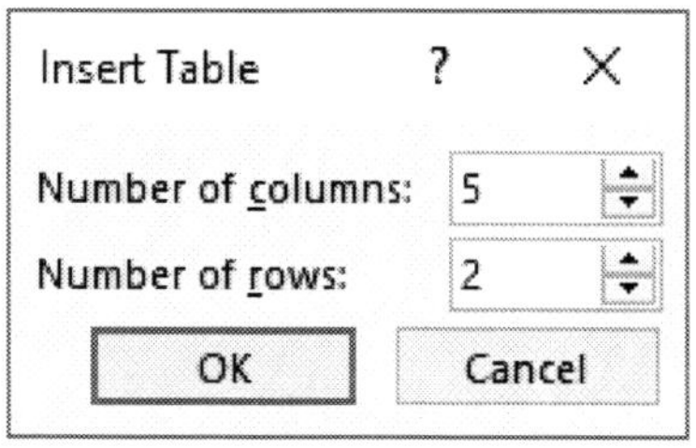

Figure 6-3: The fields in the Insert Table dialog box.

Table Navigation Methods

You have several options for navigating the cells in your tables. Navigating from cell to cell allows you to enter data and other information where you need it. You can activate a cell by selecting it with the cursor, or you can navigate from cell to cell by using the keyboard. Once you have selected a cell, you can use the keyboard to enter textual content.

Navigation Action	Keystroke
Move one cell to the right	**Tab** or the **Right Arrow** key
Move one cell to the left	**Shift+Tab** or the **Left Arrow** key
Move down one cell	**Down Arrow** key

Navigation Action	Keystroke
Move up one cell	**Up Arrow** key

	Access the Checklist tile on your CHOICE Course screen for reference information and job aids on How to Create a Table.

ACTIVITY 6-1
Creating a Table

Data Files

C:\091060Data\Adding Tables to Your Presentation\Develetech Ind_Tables.pptx

C:\091060Data\Adding Tables to Your Presentation\Sales Projections.xls

Before You Begin

Microsoft Excel 2016 is installed.

Scenario

Your supervisor has informed you that the VP of product development has asked that sales projections for the new product line be included in the presentation to generate excitement over the launch. You decide to add a table to display previous product sales figures next to the projections for the new product line.

---

1. Create a new slide for the table.
   a) From the **C:\091060Data\Adding Tables to Your Presentation** folder, open the **Develetech Ind_Tables.pptx** file.
   b) Navigate to slide **13**.
   c) Select **Home→Slides→New Slide** down arrow, and from the drop-down menu that appears, select **Title Only**.
   d) In the new slide, in the title text placeholder, type *Sales Projections*
   e) Click outside the title text placeholder to deselect it.

2. Insert a table on the slide.
   a) Select **Insert→Tables→Table→Insert Table**.
   b) In the **Insert Table** dialog box, in the **Number of columns** text box, replace the existing value with *4*
   c) In the **Number of rows** text box, replace the existing value with *6* and then select **OK**.
   d) In the first row of the table, starting from the first cell in the left, type the text as given in the image.

Product	Previous Version Sales $M	Projected Sales $M	Over/Under %

 Note: Press the **Tab** key to navigate to the next cell in the row.

e) In the first column titled "Product," starting from the first cell in the second row, type the text as given in the image.

Product	Previous Version Sales $M	Projected Sales $M	Over/Under %
Knomatico			
GeoExis			
Handia			
Melius			
Protoi			

> **Note:** Press the **Down Arrow** key to navigate to the next cell in the column.

3. Copy the data required for the table.

   a) In File Explorer, from the **C:\091060Data\Adding Tables to Your Presentation** folder, open the **Sales Projections.xlsx** file.

   b) In the Excel worksheet, select cell **B2** and drag the cursor down to cell **D6**.

   c) Select **Home→Clipboard→Copy**.

4. Populate the table with the copied data.

   a) Switch to the PowerPoint window and select the second cell in the second row of the table.

   b) Select **Home→Clipboard→Paste**.

Product	Previous Version Sales $M	Projected Sales $M	Over/Under %
Knomatico	121.2	218.1	+80
GeoExis	345.7	473.6	+37
Handia	98.6	110.4	+12
Melius	203.1	221.4	+9
Protoi	78.2	87.6	+12

Sales Projections

   c) Save the file to the **C:\091060Data\Adding Tables to Your Presentation** folder as *My Develetech Ind_Tables.pptx*

5. Close the Microsoft Excel window.

TOPIC B

Format a Table

You have created the table you need for your presentation, and you have entered all of the data you need to convey to the audience. But tables can be a bit tricky to read, especially tables that have long columns of numerical figures. You'll want to enhance your tables to make them easier for the audience to read. You will also want to make your tables mesh well with the rest of your presentation. Unformatted tables look dull, and they may not blend well with the other elements of a highly stylized presentation.

PowerPoint 2016 gives you a wide range of options for formatting the tables in your presentations. You can use the table formatting options to enhance the clarity and the visual appeal of your tables. You can also add graphical elements to your tables, rather than relying solely on figures and other textual content.

The Table Tools Contextual Tab

When you create a table in PowerPoint 2016, the **Table Tools** contextual tab is displayed automatically. The **Table Tools** contextual tab is divided between the **Design** and the **Layout** tabs. These tabs contain all of the commands associated with formatting and modifying tables.

 Note: PowerPoint Online App

The table design and layout tools are available in a scaled-down version, but they function the same as discussed here.

The Design Tab

The **Design** tab in the **Table Tools** contextual tab gives you access to the various commands that you will use to format the overall look of your tables.

Design Tab Group	Provides Commands For
Table Style Options	Highlighting particular areas of your tables to enhance clarity. For example, alternate rows or columns can be shaded with different colors to make the table easier to read.
Table Styles	Formatting the overall look of your tables. You can use the commands in the **Table Styles** group to add shading to cells, modify the look of borders, or apply graphical effects to your tables.
WordArt Styles	Adding or modifying WordArt.
Draw Borders	Drawing in or erasing columns and rows, and modifying the style, size, and color of borders and other gridlines.

The Layout Tab

The **Layout** tab in the **Table Tools** contextual tab gives you access to the various commands that you will use to format the structure of your tables.

Layout Tab Group	Provides Commands For
Table	Displaying the gridlines within tables and selecting areas of tables for formatting.

Layout Tab Group	Provides Commands For
Rows & Columns	Adding or deleting rows and columns.
Merge	Merging or splitting cells.
Cell Size	Modifying the size of cells in a table.
Alignment	Aligning the text within cells.
Table Size	Modifying the size of the table.
Arrange	Arranging graphical objects within cells, and arranging the table in relation to other objects.

 Note: Arranging objects was covered in depth in a previous lesson.

Table Styles

As with many other features in PowerPoint 2016, you can quickly apply pre-formatted styles to your tables. The **Table Styles** gallery provides you with an array of Quick Styles that you can apply to the tables in your presentations.

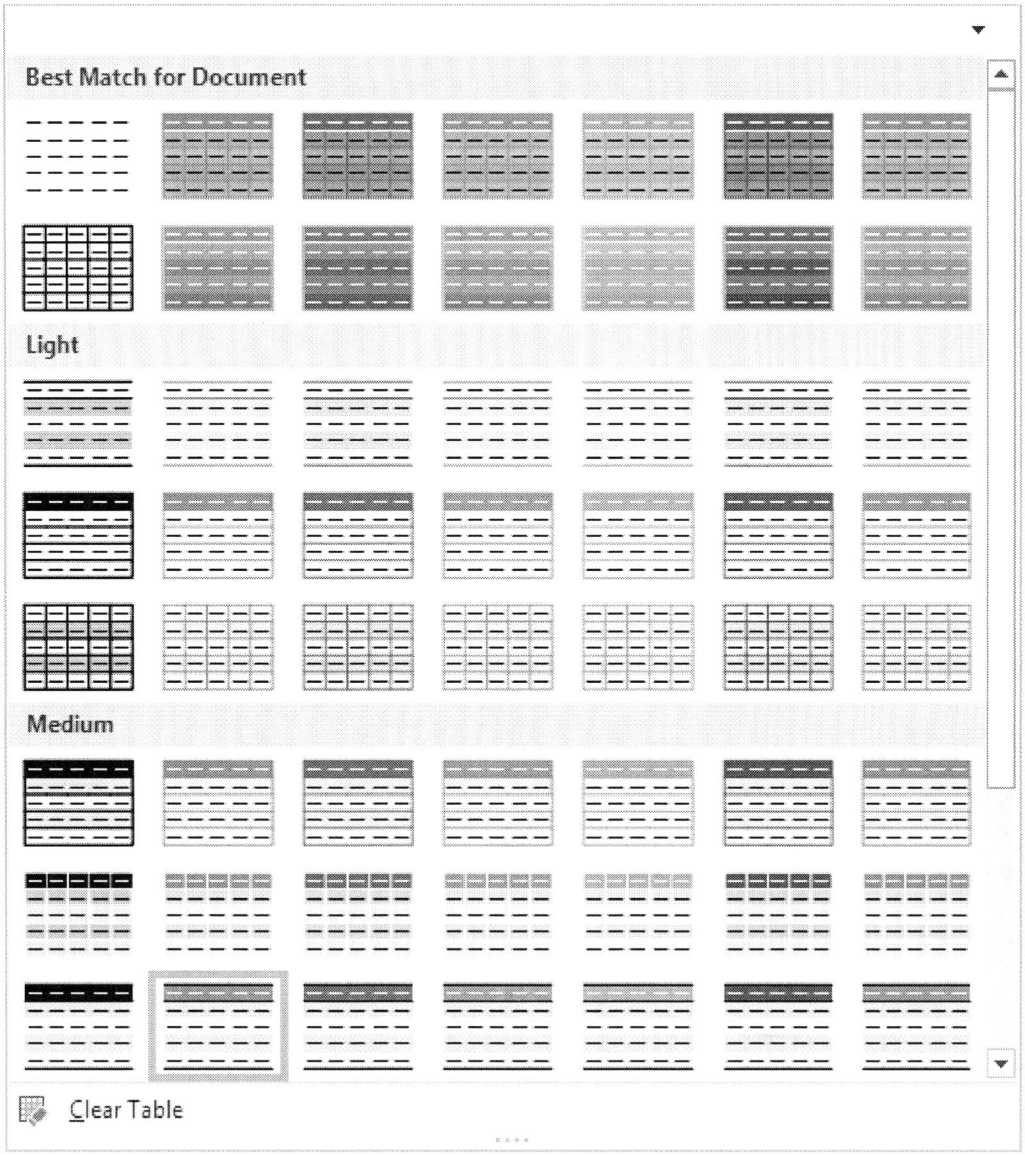

Figure 6-4: Pre-formatted styles in the Table Styles gallery.

Table Fill Options

As with other objects in your presentation, PowerPoint 2016 gives you the ability to customize the backgrounds of cells and tables. PowerPoint provides several shading options that you can use to apply fills to your tables. In addition to solid color backgrounds, gradient, texture, and picture fills are available for formatting cells and tables.

Note: Formatting fills was covered in depth in previous lessons.

Access the Checklist tile on your CHOICE Course screen for reference information and job aids on How to Format a Table.

ACTIVITY 6-2
Formatting a Table

Before You Begin
The file My Develetech Ind_Tables.pptx is open.

Scenario
You have added the sales figures to the table in the presentation. As the table is fairly small relative to the slide, you decide to scale up the table to better fill the slide. You also decide to enhance the look of the table so that the text and numbers are easily readable.

1. Resize the table.
   a) In slide **14**, select the table and on the **Table Tools** contextual tab, select the **Layout** tab.
   b) In the **Table Size** group, check the **Lock Aspect Ratio** check box.
   c) In the **Height** spin box, select the up arrow button several times to increase the height of the table to **4"**.

2. Align the table.
   a) On the **View** tab, in the **Show** group, check the **Guides** check box.
   b) Move the cursor over the table until it appears with the **Move** cursor ⁺↕⁺, and then drag the table so that it is centered on the slide and positioned above the title text.
   c) On the **View** tab, in the **Show** group, uncheck the **Guides** check box.

3. Add formatting to the table.
   a) If necessary, select the table.
   b) On the **Home** tab, in the **Font** group, from the **Font Size** drop-down list, select **20**.
   c) On the **Table Tools** contextual tab, select the **Design** tab.
   d) In the **Table Styles** group, select the **More** button. ⤓
   e) In the gallery, in the **Medium** section, select **Medium Style 3 - Accent 1**, which is the second tile in the third row.

4. Align text within the table.
   a) Select the top row within the table by selecting the **Product** cell, pressing and holding down the **Shift** key, and then selecting the **Over/Under %** cell.
   b) On the **Table Tools** contextual tab, select **Layout→Alignment→Center**. ≡
   c) Select **Layout→Alignment→Center Vertically**. ▤

5. Align the values in the last column.
   a) Select values of the last column within the table by selecting the cell with the value **+80**, pressing and holding the **Shift** key, and then selecting the cell with the value **+12**.

b) On the **Table Tools** contextual tab, select **Layout→Alignment→Align Right**. ☰

Product	Previous Version Sales $M	Projected Sales $M	Over/Under %
Knomatico	121.2	218.1	+80
GeoExis	345.7	473.6	+37
Handia	98.6	110.4	+12
Melius	203.1	221.4	+9
Protoi	78.2	87.6	+12

Sales Projections

6. Save the changes to the file.

TOPIC C

Insert a Table from Other Microsoft Office Applications

You can now create tables within your presentations to clearly display figures and other textual information. However, entering numbers into large tables can be a tedious, time-consuming process. And copying large amounts of data manually can lead to mistakes. In such a situation, you will often already have the tables you need for your presentations in other documents. Recreating that work is simply a waste of time.

PowerPoint 2016 gives you the ability to import tables from Microsoft Word and Microsoft Excel® into your presentations. By importing existing tables, you can save the development effort and reduce potential errors. This option also facilitates a consistent look and feel across documentation for large projects.

 Note: PowerPoint Online App
The features covered in this topic are only available in PowerPoint 2016.

Linking vs. Embedding

There are two methods for importing objects from other files in PowerPoint: *linking* and *embedding*. The main difference between a linked object and an embedded object is in the location where the data is stored. When you link an object to a slide in your presentation, the data is stored in the source file. When the object is updated in the source file, the changes will reflect in your presentation. Linking objects is a good option when another person is responsible for updating the document and you want the changes reflected in your presentation, and when file size is a concern.

When you embed an object in your presentation, you are placing a copy of the data in the PowerPoint file. The object becomes a part of your presentation file and is no longer connected to the source file. Changes in the source file will not be reflected in your presentation.

The Insert Object Dialog Box

The **Insert Object** dialog box allows you to insert an object or text from another file into your presentation. You can choose to create the content in a new file by selecting an application, or to browse through your computer for a file from which to insert an object or text. You can also indicate if you are linking or embedding the content by using the **Link** check box.

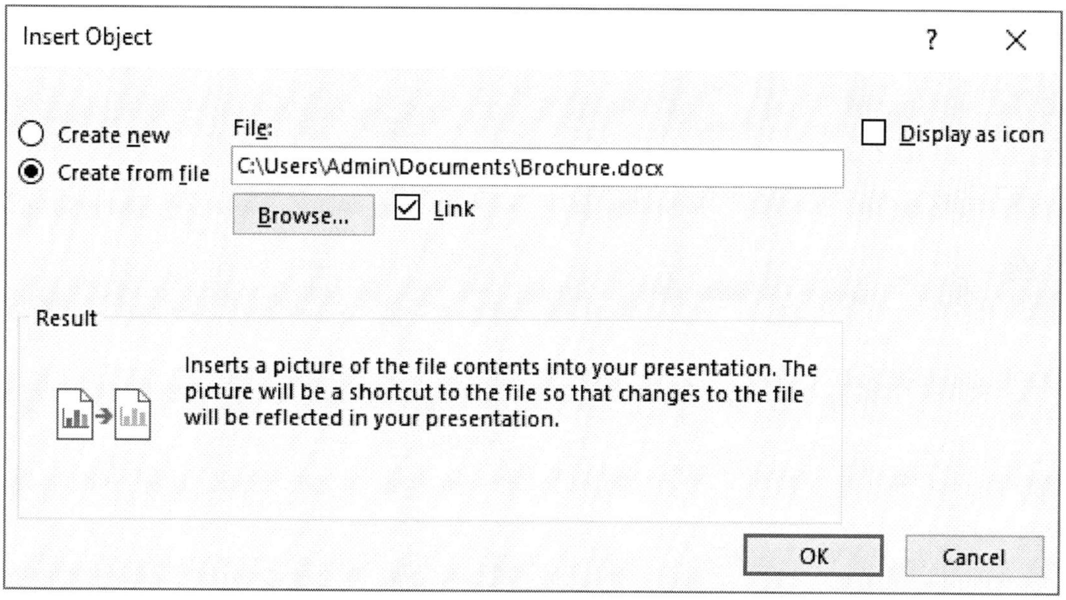

Figure 6-5: Options in the Insert Object dialog box.

> **Access the Checklist tile on your CHOICE Course screen for reference information and job aids on How to Insert Tables from Other Microsoft Office Applications.**

ACTIVITY 6–3
Inserting a Microsoft Excel Worksheet

Data File

C:\091060Data\Adding Tables to Your Presentation\New Visions Now Contacts.xlsx

Before You Begin

The file My Develetech Ind_Tables.pptx is open.

Scenario

As the presentation is nearly ready for delivery, you have asked several people to review the content. You have received multiple requests from the reviewers to include a list of important contacts for the project teams associated with the various new projects. Another member of your development team has an existing Microsoft Excel worksheet with all of the contacts. You ask him to send it to you so that you can include it in the presentation. You decide to link the Excel file to the presentation so that any future changes will need to be made in only one document.

1. Create a new slide for the worksheet.
   a) If necessary, navigate to slide **14**.
   b) Select **Home→Slides→New Slide** down arrow, and from the drop-down menu that appears, select **Title Only**.
   c) In the new slide, in the title text placeholder, type *Who's Who?*
   d) Click outside the title text placeholder to deselect it.

2. Link the Excel worksheet to the slide.
   a) Select **Insert→Text→Object**.
   b) In the **Insert Object** dialog box, select the **Create from file** option, and then select **Browse**.
   c) In the **Browse** dialog box, navigate to the **C:\091060Data\Adding Tables to Your Presentation** folder.
   d) Select the **New Visions Now Contacts.xlsx** file and then select **OK**.
   e) In the **Insert Object** dialog box, check the **Link** check box, and then select **OK**.

3. Resize and reposition the object.
   a) If necessary, select the object that displays the linked Excel worksheet.
   b) On the **Drawing Tools** contextual tab, on the **Format** tab, in the **Size** group, in the **Shape Height** text box, replace the existing value with *4.2* and press **Enter**.

c) Move the cursor over the object until it appears with the **Move** cursor, and then drag the object so that it is centered on the slide and positioned above the title text.

 Note: You cannot format the individual cells within the linked table because it is inserted as a shape. The inserted object in the PowerPoint slide appears with the same formatting options applied to the table in Excel.

Product	Project Manager	Lead Designer	Dept. Director	Business Engagement Manager
Knomatico	Ava Giroux	Frank Pendleton	MaryJo Peters	Jackson Myers
GeoExis	Dietrich Brown	Kim Chan	Alex McDonald	Avery Billups
Handia	Mark Sanders	Andrew Zacker	Garnetta Day	Su Mahley
Melius	Daj Vasica	Pau VanWaart	Joann Nash	Jam Kanish
Protoi	Samantha Erne	Ellis Yandow	Carl Gatica	Mandy Eberly

Who's Who?

4. Save the changes and close the file.

Summary

In this lesson, you added tables to your presentation to convey large amounts of numerical data to your audience. Your tables are formatted so that they are easy to read and fit well with the overall look of your presentation.

What are some creative uses for tables that you will be able to include in a variety of presentations?

What advantages, not already discussed, are there to using existing tables and worksheets in presentations?

 Note: Check your CHOICE Course screen for opportunities to interact with your classmates, peers, and the larger CHOICE online community about the topics covered in this course or other topics you are interested in. From the Course screen you can also access available resources for a more continuous learning experience.

7 Adding Charts to Your Presentation

Lesson Time: 35 minutes

Lesson Introduction

It is sometimes difficult for an audience to grasp the meaning of large amounts of data or financial information just by glancing over tables. This is especially true for long tables that have many columns. In larger rooms, it may be difficult for some audience members to see such figures on the screen. You typically don't have the time available during a presentation for people to spend analyzing complex tables. And, quite frankly, that can make for a boring presentation. You need a way to quickly show the audience members why all of this information matters to them.

Microsoft® Office PowerPoint® 2016 provides you with the ability to create eye-catching charts that show the meaning behind complex strings of data. You have a vast array of options for formatting these charts to make your point clearly, and to show the audience a broader view of the data. Using these features lends visual appeal to your presentations and reduces the amount of time you need to spend explaining complex numerical relationships.

Lesson Objectives

In this lesson, you will:

- Create a chart.

- Format a chart.

- Insert a chart from Microsoft Excel.

TOPIC A

Create a Chart

You have added tables to your presentation, and these tables contain information about sales trends, research findings, or other key matters. To most of the audience, all that matters is the impact of this information. You may need to convert the data in your tables into charts that your audience can analyze and interpret instantly.

Charts help you visually represent numerical information to your audience. You can create a variety of charts in PowerPoint 2016, which allows you to tailor charts to best suit the specific needs of your presentation.

> **Note: PowerPoint Online App**
>
> Using the online app, you cannot insert a chart. However, any charts that were inserted in PowerPoint 2016 will be displayed as pictures in **Editing** view.

Charts

Charts are graphical representations of numerical or mathematical data. You can use charts to display the relationships among groups of numbers from spreadsheets and tables. In PowerPoint 2016, charts may also contain titles, legends, and a data table.

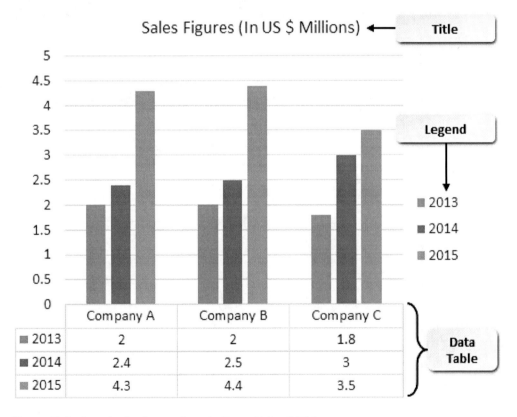

Figure 7–1: A typical column chart in PowerPoint 2016.

Chart Data

When you insert a chart into your presentation, PowerPoint automatically launches a Microsoft Excel® worksheet in a separate window containing sample data that will populate the chart. The sample data worksheet contains labels for the columns and rows. These labels appear in a preview of the chart on the slide. You can change the labels and the data to suit your needs. You can also add rows or columns to the worksheet. The chart automatically reflects the changes as you make them. Although the worksheet opens in Excel, there is no separate Excel file. The data for the chart is contained within, and saved along with, the PowerPoint file.

 Note: The data worksheet opens in a limited-functionality Excel environment. However, once you have created the chart, PowerPoint 2016 gives you the option of editing the chart data in the full version of Excel 2016.

	A	B	C	D	E	F
1		2013	2014	2015		
2	Company A	2	2.4	4.3		
3	Company B	2	2.5	4.4		
4	Company C	1.8	3	3.5		
5						

Figure 7-2: Sample chart data in PowerPoint 2016.

The Switch Row/Column Feature

You can switch the rows and the columns of chart data between axes by using the *Switch Row/ Column* feature. This feature allows you to change the orientation of information along the X and the Y axes without having to re-enter your data. The data that is charted along the X axis becomes the data charted along the Y axis and vice versa.

 Note: The Switch Row/Column feature is disabled when the Excel worksheet containing the chart data is closed.

The Insert Chart Dialog Box

The **Insert Chart** dialog box allows you to select the best chart type and subtype for your presentation. PowerPoint 2016 offers you fifteen types of charts for use in your presentations. The type of chart you use will depend on the type of information you wish to convey, as each is well-suited to particular uses. Most of the fifteen chart types contain a gallery of chart subtypes.

PowerPoint 2016 includes six new chart types, namely, Treemap, Sunburst, Histogram and Pareto, Box and Whisker, and Waterfall.

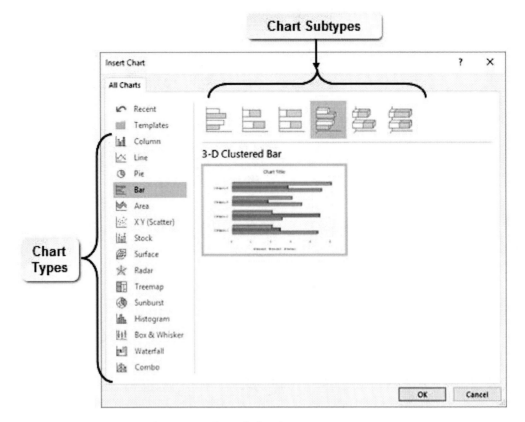

Figure 7-3: Options in the Insert Chart dialog box.

Chart Types

The chart types in PowerPoint enable you to visually represent different kinds of data. The table describes some of the most commonly used chart types and the new chart types available in PowerPoint 2016.

Chart Type	Is Used for Plotting Data
Column	That is arranged in columns and rows in tables and spreadsheets. Column charts are useful for plotting data changes over time, and for making comparisons. Column charts typically contain categories along the X axis and numerical figures along the Y axis.
Line	That is arranged in columns and rows in tables and spreadsheets. Line charts are ideal for illustrating trends over time.
Pie	From a single column or row. Pie charts are useful for displaying values as a percentage of the whole.
Bar	That is arranged in columns and rows. Bar charts are best suited to making comparisons among items.
Treemap	That is organized as a hierarchy. A treemap chart segregates categories using color, shows their relationship with one another, and indicates ratios within the hierarchy. Treemap charts are best suited for comparison of hierarchical views of data.
Sunburst	That is organized as a hierarchical structure with gaps in the hierarchy. A sunburst chart is made up of concentric rings with each ring representing one level of hierarchy. Sunburst charts are ideal for displaying data organized in multiple levels of categories.

Chart Type	Is Used for Plotting Data
Histogram	That is arranged over a distribution. In a histogram chart, the columns represent data ranges in the form of frequency bins and the vertical bars show the frequency distribution. Histogram charts are best suited to display frequencies in a distribution of data.
Pareto	That is arranged over a sorted distribution. Pareto chart is a subtype of the Histogram chart type that displays sorted histogram charts in which the columns are sorted in descending order. These charts also display a cumulative total percentage value as a line.
Box & Whisker	That includes multiple data sets. A box and whisker chart indicates mean values and outliers in a distribution of data. While a box shows data distribution, a whisker shows variation of data in the upper and lower quartiles. Box and whisker charts are ideal for presenting multiple data sets that are related to one another.
Waterfall	That includes both positive and negative values. A waterfall chart displays running totals of data and shows how a value is affected by the inclusion of positive and negative values. Waterfall charts are ideal for analyzing fluctuations in financial data.

Access the Checklist tile on your CHOICE Course screen for reference information and job aids on How to Create a Chart.

ACTIVITY 7-1
Creating a Chart

Data File

C:\091060Data\Adding Charts to Your Presentation\Develetech Ind_Charts.pptx

Scenario

You realize that a visual representation of the projected sales growth for the new product line would make a big impact on Develetech employees at the product launch meetings. You decide to use a chart to visually demonstrate the company's projected sales increases due to the new product rollouts.

1. Open a presentation.
   a) From the **C:\091060Data\Adding Charts to Your Presentation** folder, open the **Develetech Ind_Charts.pptx** file.
   b) When prompted, in the **Microsoft PowerPoint Security Notice** dialog box, select **Update Links**.

2. Insert a chart.
   a) Navigate to slide **14**.
   b) Select **Home→Slides→New Slide** down-arrow, and from the drop-down menu that appears, select **Blank**.
   c) In the new slide, select **Insert→Illustrations→Chart**.
   d) In the **Insert Chart** dialog box, in the left pane, ensure that the **Column** chart type is selected, and in the right pane, ensure that the **Clustered Column** subtype is selected.
   e) Select **OK**.

3. Edit the chart data.
   a) In the **Chart in Microsoft PowerPoint** window, move the cursor to the bottom-right corner of cell **D5**, and when the cursor changes to a double-headed arrow, drag down and left to cell **C6**.

    Note: In the chart data, the data range is indicated by a blue border, the categories range by a purple border, and the series range by a brown border.

	A	B	C	D	E
1		Series 1	Series 2	Series 3	
2	Category 1	4.3	2.4	2	
3	Category 2	2.5	4.4	2	
4	Category 3	3.5	1.8	3	
5	Category 4	4.5	2.8	5	
6					
7					

   b) Select cell **B1** and type *Previous Version Sales $M* and then select cell **C1** and type *Projected Sales $M*

4. Copy data from a slide.

a) Navigate to slide **14**.

b) Select the cell with the text "Knomatico," hold down **Shift**, and select the third cell in the last row with the value "87.6."

c) Copy the contents of the selected cells.

5. Paste the copied data.

a) Navigate to slide 15.

b) In the **Chart in Microsoft PowerPoint** window, select cell **A2**.

c) Right-click, and in the **Paste Options** section, select **Match Destination Formatting**.

6. Complete the changes to the data worksheet.

a) Right-click cell **D1** and select **Delete→Table Columns**.

b) Ensure that the changes to the data are reflected in the chart and close the data worksheet.

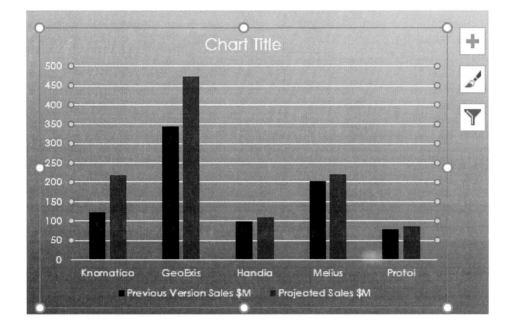

7. Save the file to the **C:\091060Data\Adding Charts to Your Presentation** folder as *My Develetech Ind_Charts.pptx*

TOPIC B

Format a Chart

Your presentation now contains charts to graphically display information from your tables and spreadsheets. But you may not have selected the best chart type or chart subtype to convey that information to the audience. Or, you may feel that the charts need some tweaking to make certain key points stand out.

PowerPoint 2016 provides you with a host of options for formatting the charts in your presentations. You can also save chart formatting as a template for creating future charts. Becoming more adept at customizing your charts will give you the ability to create simple, clean charts to illustrate even the most complex of numerical relationships.

 Note: PowerPoint Online App

In **Editing** view, charts that were inserted in PowerPoint 2016 are not editable.

The Chart Tools Contextual Tab

The **Chart Tools** contextual tab contains many of the commands you will use to edit and format your charts. This contextual tab is displayed when you select a chart in a presentation, and it is divided into two tabs: the **Design** tab and the **Format** tab.

The Design Tab

The **Design** tab on the **Chart Tools** contextual tab contains the commands you will use to modify the overall style of your charts and to edit the chart data. The following table lists the groups in the **Design** tab and describes the commands they contain.

Design Tab Group	Provides Commands For
Chart Layouts	Selecting various chart layouts. The layout of a chart determines which elements, such as titles, legends, and labels, appear on the chart.
Chart Styles	Applying style elements, such as colors, backgrounds, and effects, to your charts.
Data	Editing the chart data.
Type	Changing the chart type of a chart in your presentation.

The Format Tab

The **Format** tab on the **Chart Tools** contextual tab contains the commands you will use to change the appearance of objects on your charts. The following table lists the groups in the **Format** tab and describes the commands they contain.

Format Tab Group	Provides Commands For
Current Selection	Formatting the selected object. The **Current Selection** group also indicates the object that is currently selected.
Insert Shapes	Adding shapes to your charts, and modifying shapes contained in your charts.
Shape Styles	Applying style elements to objects in your charts.

Format Tab Group	Provides Commands For
WordArt Styles	Applying WordArt styles to chart text, such as labels and titles.
Arrange	Arranging and aligning objects on your charts.
Size	Resizing objects on your charts.

Quick Access Chart Commands

When you insert a chart into your presentation, or when you select a chart, PowerPoint 2016 displays three buttons that provide you with quick access to some of the commands you can use to format your charts: the **Chart Elements** button, the **Chart Styles** button, and the **Chart Filters** button. Many of the options you can access using the quick access chart commands are also available on the ribbon.

Quick Access Chart Command Button	Provides Commands For
Chart Elements ✚	Displaying or hiding chart elements, such as labels, titles, and gridlines.
Chart Styles 🖌	Applying style or color modifications to your charts.
Chart Filters ▼	Filtering your charts to display only certain information, such as turning off certain data series or categories, or removing labels from series or categories.

Chart Layouts

Chart Layouts determine which chart elements, such as labels, titles, and legends, will appear, and where they appear on your charts. PowerPoint 2016 provides a set of pre-formatted chart layouts, called *quick layouts*, for each type of chart. PowerPoint also gives you the ability to customize chart layouts by formatting individual chart elements.

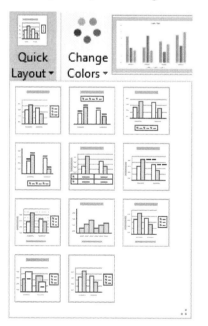

Figure 7–4: The Quick Layout gallery for a Clustered Column chart.

Chart Styles

Chart styles are quick styles that you can apply to charts. Chart styles determine the color of objects and backgrounds, and may contain effects. PowerPoint also gives you the ability to customize chart styles by applying style elements to objects and backgrounds individually.

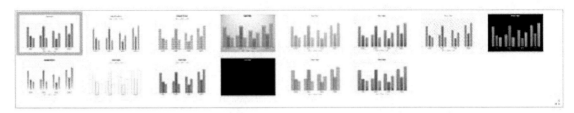

Figure 7-5: The Chart Styles gallery.

 Access the Checklist tile on your **CHOICE** Course screen for reference information and job aids on **How to Format a Chart.**

ACTIVITY 7-2
Formatting a Chart

Before You Begin
The file My Develetech Ind_Charts.pptx is open.

Scenario
After adding the chart to the presentation, you decide you don't like the type of chart you selected. You feel it looks too flat on the slide, and so you decide to change the type of chart to one of the 3-D chart types and add some formatting. You also notice the chart is not properly titled, so you will have to add it.

---

1. **Change the chart to another chart type.**
   a) In slide **15**, select the chart.
   b) On the **Chart Tools** contextual tab, select **Design→Type→Change Chart Type**.
   c) In the **Change Chart Type** dialog box, in the left pane, ensure that **Column** is selected.
   d) In the right pane, from the gallery of chart subtypes at the top, select **3-D Clustered Column**, which is the fourth chart subtype.
   e) Select **OK**.

   > **Note:** Ensure that the chart on the slide has changed.

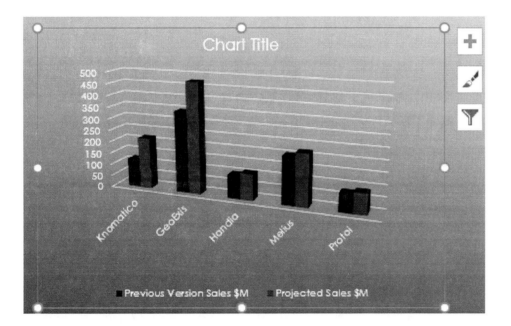

2. **Modify the chart title.**
   a) On the **Chart Tools** contextual tab, select the **Format** tab.
   b) In the **Current Selection** group, from the **Chart Elements** `Chart Area` ▾ drop-down list, select **Chart Title**.

---

c) On the chart, in the title text box, replace the text "Chart Title" with *Sales Projections*

d) Click outside the text box to deselect it.

3. Modify the layout of the chart.

a) If necessary, select the chart.

b) On the **Chart Tools** contextual tab, select **Design**→**Chart Layouts**→**Add Chart Element**→**Legend**→**Left** to move the legend to the left of the chart.

c) Select **Design**→**Chart Layouts**→**Add Chart Element**→**Gridlines**→**Primary Minor Horizontal**.

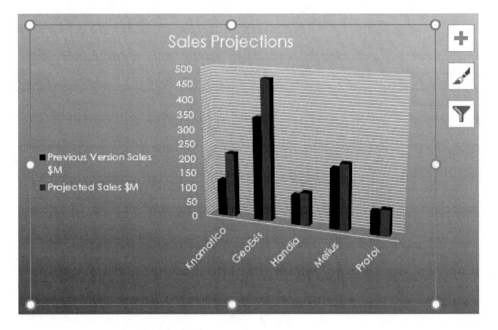

4. Modify the colors used in the chart.

a) Select **Design**→**Chart Styles**→**Change Colors**.

b) From the gallery, in the **Colorful** section, select **Color 2**, which is the second set of colors in the list.

5. Format the back wall of the chart.

a) On the **Format** tab, in the **Current Selection** group, from the **Chart Elements** drop-down list, select **Back Wall**.

b) Select **Format**→**Current Selection**→**Format Selection**.

c) In the **Format Wall** pane, ensure that the **Fill & Line** tab is selected, and then expand the **Fill** section.

d) Select the **Gradient fill** option.

e) Select the **Color** button.

f) From the gallery, in the **Theme Colors** section, select **Red, Accent 6, Lighter 80%**, which is the second tile in the last column.

6. Format the side wall of the chart.

a) On the **Format** tab, in the **Current Selection** group, from the **Chart Elements** drop-down list, select **Side Wall**.

b) In the **Format Wall** pane, select the **Gradient Fill** option.

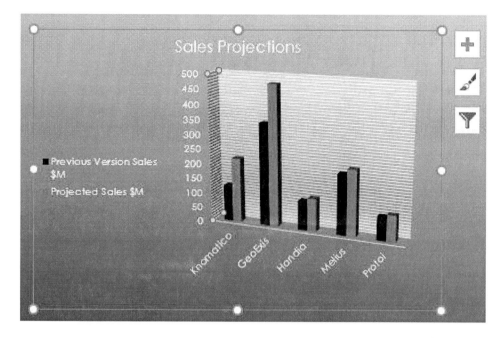

7. Reposition the chart on the slide.

a) On the **Format** tab, in the **Current Selection** group, from the **Chart Elements** drop-down list, select **Chart Area**.

b) In the **Format Chart Area** pane, select the **Size & Properties** tab.

c) Expand the **Position** section.

d) In the **Vertical position** field, in the spin box, select the up arrow button several times to set the value to **1.8**.

e) Close the **Format Chart Area** pane.

8. Save the file.

TOPIC C

Insert a Chart from Microsoft Excel

You can now create a vast array of charts to quickly illustrate the meaning behind large amounts of numerical data. While there are clear benefits to utilizing the chart functionality in PowerPoint 2016, as with tables, there is no point in duplicating work you have already performed. Let's face it, it takes time to create, populate, and format a chart that will make an impact. If you have created one already, there is no need to spend the time doing it again.

PowerPoint 2016 lets you insert existing Microsoft Excel charts to your presentations. Linking existing charts to your PowerPoint presentations offers the same benefits as using existing tables. You will save time and effort, avoid data errors, and facilitate a consistent look across various documents.

Note: PowerPoint Online App

Inserting charts from Microsoft Excel is not available in the online app. You must use PowerPoint 2016.

Linking vs. Embedding Charts

PowerPoint provides options that enable you to link and embed existing charts from Microsoft Excel into a presentation. Linking and embedding charts works the same way as linking and embedding tables. When you link a chart to a slide in a presentation, the chart is updated whenever the source is updated. However, when you embed a chart in a slide, the chart is no longer connected to the source file.

Access the Checklist tile on your CHOICE Course screen for reference information and job aids on How to Insert a Chart from Microsoft Excel.

ACTIVITY 7-3
Inserting a Chart From Microsoft Excel

Data File

C:\091060Data\Adding Charts to Your Presentation\Develetech Market Share.xlsx

Before You Begin

The file My Develetech Ind_Charts.pptx is open.

Scenario

You have received an additional request from the VP of product development. He has asked your supervisor to have you include two existing pie charts that he put together. The charts show Develetech's market share from the previous product line, and the projected company market share from the new product rollout. You decide to link the charts to the presentation so that any changes to the projections can be easily reflected in the presentation.

---

1. Insert new slides into the presentation.
   a) If necessary, navigate to slide **15**.
   b) Insert two new blank slides.

2. Link an existing chart to the presentation.
   a) In File Explorer, from the **C:\091060Data\Adding Charts to Your Presentation** folder, open the **Develetech Market Share.xlsx** file.
   b) In the Microsoft Excel window, select the chart titled **Previous Market Share**, and select **Home→Clipboard→Copy**.
   c) Switch to the presentation, and then navigate to slide **16**.

d) Select **Home→Clipboard→Paste** down arrow, and from the **Paste Options** drop-down menu, select **Use Destination Theme & Link Data**.

3. **Link another chart to the presentation.**

   a) Navigate to slide **17**.
   b) Switch to the **Develetech Market Share.xlsx** file in Microsoft Excel.
   c) Scroll down and select the chart titled **Projected Market Share**, and then copy it to the clipboard.
   d) Switch back to the presentation.
   e) Select **Home→Clipboard→Paste** down arrow, and from the **Paste Options** drop-down menu, select **Use Destination Theme & Link Data**.

4. **Save and close the PowerPoint file.**

5. **Close the Microsoft Excel 2016 window.**

Summary

In this lesson, you added charts and your PowerPoint presentation is now complete! You have developed a truly engaging multimedia presentation that will help you deliver your message and make a big impact on the audience.

In your daily life, where do you most often encounter charts that are being used to make sense of numerical information? Why are they used in these instances?

Which do you think you will use in your presentations more, charts or tables? Why?

 Note: Check your CHOICE Course screen for opportunities to interact with your classmates, peers, and the larger CHOICE online community about the topics covered in this course or other topics you are interested in. From the Course screen you can also access available resources for a more continuous learning experience.

8 | Preparing to Deliver Your Presentation

Lesson Time: 40 minutes

Lesson Introduction

Congratulations! You are ready to deliver your presentation. Or rather, you're almost ready to deliver it. You have a clear message that is well-organized, and one that you have supported with images and numerical data. However, nothing kills credibility like glaring mistakes on your slides as you deliver your presentation. You will want to review and polish your work before stepping up to the podium. Additionally, there may be particular considerations you need to address for your specific situation. Does the audience require handouts? Will you need to archive or share your presentation after the event?

Microsoft® Office PowerPoint® 2016 provides you with a variety of options for reviewing, revising, printing, and presenting your work. Becoming familiar with these functions will help you transform your presentation from a file on a computer, to a real-life event that makes an impact on your audience.

Lesson Objectives

In this lesson, you will prepare to deliver your presentation. You will:

- Review your presentation.

- Apply transitions.

- Print your presentation.

- Deliver your presentation.

TOPIC A

Review Your Presentation

It's been a while since you started adding text to your presentation. Before you get in front of a live audience, you want to make sure your text is perfect. After all, it's your credibility that is on the line. But mistakes aren't the only things that can be distracting to an audience. Have you used the same word too many times? Do you need to add some variety to your text?

PowerPoint 2016 offers you a number of tools that can help you deliver a clean, accurate presentation. Making a habit of checking your work before presenting can help you avoid some common presentation-delivery pitfalls.

Note: PowerPoint Online App

The presentation review tools that are discussed in this topic are not available in the online app. You must use PowerPoint 2016.

The AutoCorrect Feature

PowerPoint 2016 includes an *AutoCorrect feature* that corrects common spelling and capitalization errors as you type. The AutoCorrect feature also corrects common capitalization and text-formatting issues, and inserts mathematical symbols when you type the symbol names. This feature can be turned off and on, and you can adjust the AutoCorrect settings. The default state of the AutoCorrect feature is on.

The AutoCorrect Feature Options

You can customize the AutoCorrect feature by selecting the types of errors it will correct for you. The **AutoCorrect** dialog box enables you to specify options for customizing the AutoCorrect feature.

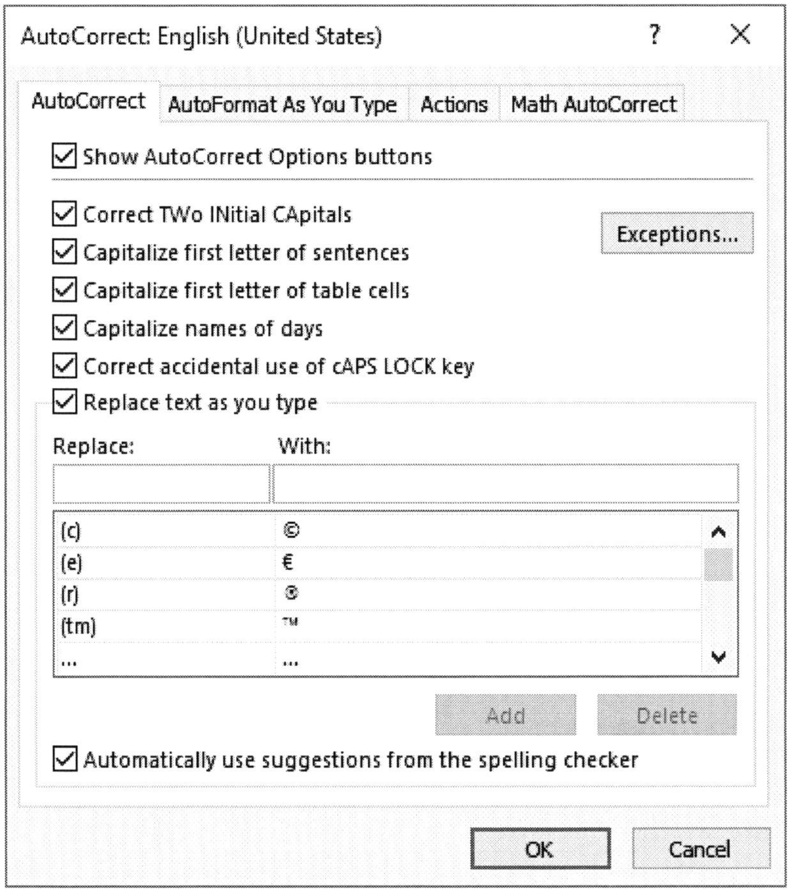

Figure 8-1: The AutoCorrect dialog box with options for customizing the AutoCorrect feature.

The following table describes options for the **AutoCorrect** dialog box tab.

AutoCorrect Dialog Box Tab	Provides Options For
AutoCorrect	Correcting spelling and capitalization errors, and correcting text typed with the **Caps Lock** key enabled.
AutoFormat As You Type	Formatting fractions and symbols, and for common text formatting like bulleted lists.
Actions	Creating additional actions for right-click menus when you type particular words.
Math AutoCorrect	Replacing typed text with mathematical symbols.

The Spelling Checker Feature

The *Spelling Checker feature* scans all of the text in your presentation looking for spelling errors. The Spelling Checker feature compares the text on your slides and in the **Notes** pane against a built-in list of words based on your language settings. Spelling errors will launch the **Spelling** pane, which gives you a set of options for how you would like PowerPoint to treat the misspelled word. The misspelled word is displayed on the slide with a text highlight.

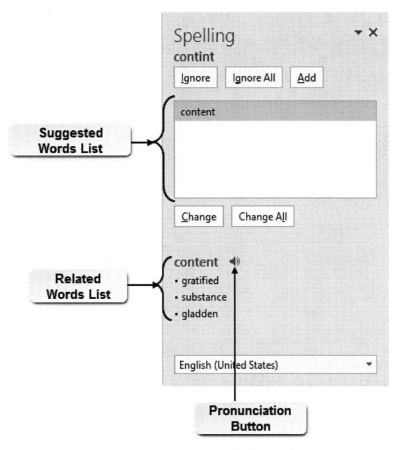

Figure 8-2: The Spelling pane with options to resolve spelling errors.

The following table describes the **Spelling** pane elements.

Spelling Pane Element	Description
Ignore button	Leaves the current instance of the misspelled word as is.
Ignore All button	Leaves all instances of the misspelled word as they are.
Add button	Adds the misspelled word to the dictionary. Once this is done, the Spelling Checker will no longer consider the word a misspelling.
Suggested words list	Displays a list of suggested replacements for the misspelled word.
Change button	Replaces the current instance of the misspelled word with the selected word in the suggested words list.
Change All button	Replaces all instances of the misspelled word with the selected word in the suggested words list.
Pronunciation button	Plays an audio file of the currently selected word in the suggested words list.
Related words list	Displays a list of synonyms for the currently selected word in the suggested words list.

The Smart Lookup Feature

The Smart Lookup feature enables you to research on specific terms in your presentation. This feature helps you to explore topics of interest by displaying web search results within PowerPoint. When you perform a Smart Lookup operation on a word or phrase, PowerPoint runs a web search using the Bing® search tool and displays the results in the **Insights** pane. The results include Wiki articles, definitions, and links to related web pages.

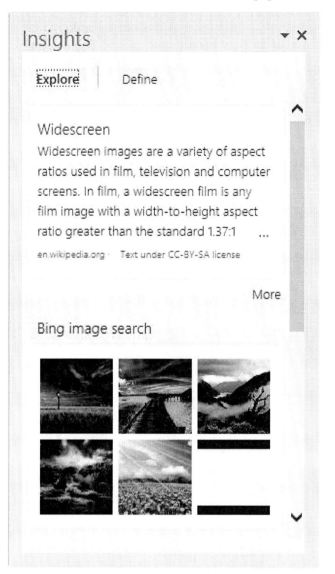

Figure 8-3: The Insights pane with web search results.

> **Note:** The **Research** pane is not available in PowerPoint 2016. Instead, you can now use the Smart Lookup feature for your research.

> **Note:** The Smart Lookup feature returns results only if you are connected to the Internet.

The Thesaurus

The *thesaurus* is a research tool that provides you with a list of synonyms and antonyms for a particular word. The thesaurus feature returns search results in the **Thesaurus** pane. By using the options in the **Thesaurus** pane, you can replace the selected word with a suitable word.

The Compatibility Checker Feature

In addition to checking your presentation for grammatical issues and errors, PowerPoint 2016 provides you with options for ensuring your presentation file is compatible with previous versions of PowerPoint, and that the content on your slides is accessible to persons with disabilities.

While the default file format for PowerPoint 2016 is the .pptx file, previous versions of PowerPoint used the PPT file format. This means, the .pptx files you create using PowerPoint 2016 may not be compatible with the 97-2003 versions of the application. And, some features of PowerPoint 2016 that were not available in or have changed since PowerPoint 2007 and PowerPoint 2010, may not function properly in the earlier version. So, PowerPoint 2016 provides you with the ability to check your presentations for compatibility issues with previous versions of PowerPoint. The Microsoft PowerPoint *Compatibility Checker* displays a list of possible compatibility issues and provides you with links to Help material to resolve them. You can access the **Microsoft PowerPoint Compatibility Checker** dialog box from the **Info** tab in the **Backstage** view.

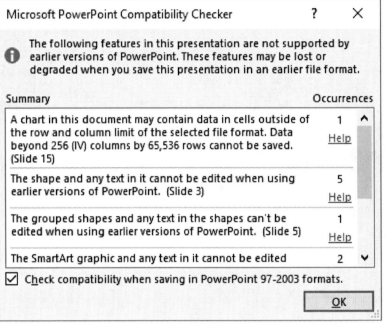

Figure 8-4: The Microsoft PowerPoint Compatibility Checker dialog box.

Note: You can save your presentation in the PPT file format by selecting **PowerPoint 97-2003 Presentation (*.ppt)** in the **Save As** dialog box when you save the file. This will allow users to open the file in previous versions of PowerPoint. Although, not all content within the file may be compatible with the previous versions.

The Accessibility Checker Feature

For some persons with disabilities, some of the content on your slides may not be fully accessible. People with vision impairment may not be able to view the images in your presentations or read the text on your slides. People who are hearing impaired may not be able to hear audio tracks or the sound from embedded video. So, PowerPoint 2016 provides you with the ability to check your presentations for possible accessibility issues. The *Accessibility Checker* displays a list of the content in your presentation that may prove difficult for some people to access, and displays additional information about the accessibility issues and provides a link to Help articles on related subjects. You can access the **Accessibility Checker** pane from the **Info** tab in the **Backstage** view.

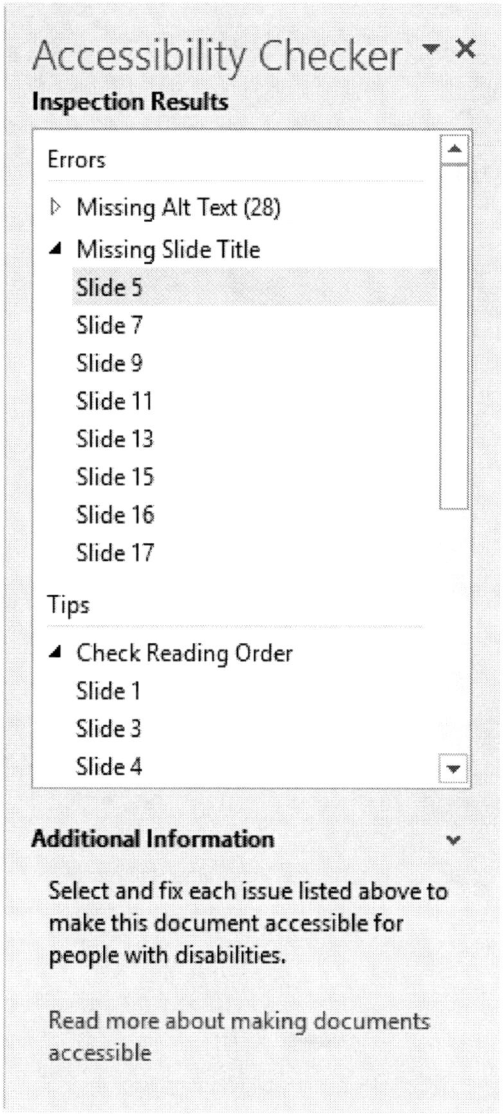

Figure 8-5: The Accessibility Checker pane with results of an inspection for accessibility issues.

> Access the Checklist tile on your CHOICE Course screen for reference information and job aids on How to Review Your Presentation.

ACTIVITY 8-1
Reviewing Your Presentations

Data File

C:\091060Data\Preparing to Deliver Your Presentation\Develetech Ind_Delivery.pptx

Scenario

You and the other members of the design team have finished adding all of the content for the presentation, and all preliminary reviews are complete. You decide it would be a good idea to check the presentation for spelling errors before submitting the presentation for final approval.

1. Run the Spelling Checker feature.
   a) From the **C:\091060Data\Preparing to Deliver Your Presentation** folder, open the **Develetech Ind_Delivery.pptx** file.
   b) Update the links when prompted.
   c) Select **Review→Proofing→Spelling**.

2. Specify settings to ignore spell check for names, pronunciation notes, and technical terms.
   a) In the **Spelling** pane, select **Ignore All** to ignore spelling for all instances of the word "Develetech."
   b) For the next error text "Handia" and for subsequent errors with the text "Protoi," "GeoExis," "Melius," and "Knomatico," select **Ignore All**.
   c) For errors in pronunciation notes and technical terms, such as "XGA," select **Ignore All**.

3. Correct spelling errors.
   a) In the **Spelling** pane, ensure that "Gaming" is the appropriate word for the highlighted text, and then select **Change**.

b) Ensure that "Networking" is the appropriate word for the highlighted text, and then select **Change**.

 Note: If the Spelling Checker highlights names, pronunciation notes, or technical terms similar to the ones you ignored earlier, select **Ignore All**.

c) In the **Microsoft PowerPoint** message box, select **OK**.

4. Research a word by using Smart Lookup.

a) Navigate to slide **2**.
b) In the third bullet point, select the text **"Web-TV"**.
c) Select **Review→Insights→Smart Lookup**.
d) In the **Insights** pane, view the information regarding privacy and select **Got It**.

e) From the web search results, select a link to view the corresponding web page.
f) Close the Microsoft Edge window.
g) Close the **Insights** pane.
h) Click anywhere outside the text "Web-TV" to deselect it.

5. Save the file to the **C:\091060Data\Preparing to Deliver Your Presentation** folder as *My Develetech Ind_Delivery.pptx*

TOPIC B

Apply Transitions

You have corrected all of the spelling and grammatical errors in your presentation. You could deliver your presentation as is and have a successful event. However, you want your presentation to really stand out. Repeatedly presenting one slide after another with no transition effects can get monotonous for the audience. You may want to add some flair to the transitions between your slides.

PowerPoint 2016 contains a host of on-board transition effects that can liven up your presentation. You can also apply slide transitions to emphasize slides that convey an important point.

Transitions

Transitions are visual effects that occur as you advance from one slide to the next in a presentation. PowerPoint 2016 includes a wide array of transition effects that you can apply to the slides in your presentation. You can modify the speed of transitions, change transition attributes such as direction or shape, and add sounds to transitions. Transitions can play automatically, respond to keystrokes or mouse clicks, or play after a specified period of time.

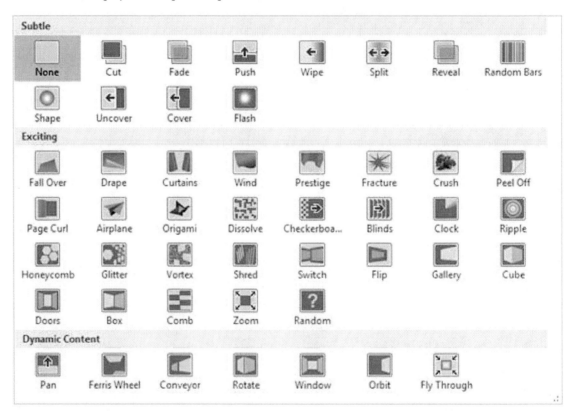

Figure 8-6: The gallery of slide transitions available in PowerPoint 2016.

> **Note:** Once you apply a transition to a slide, a star will appear next to the slide in the **Normal** and **Slide Sorter** views.

> **Note: PowerPoint Online App**

You have access to a limited number of transitions in the online app; however, all transitions that are applied in PowerPoint 2016 will be preserved when you run the slideshow online.

 Note: To further explore transitions, you can access the LearnTO **Effectively Use PowerPoint Animations and Transitions** presentation from the **LearnTO** tile on the CHOICE Course screen.

 Access the Checklist tile on your **CHOICE Course** screen for reference information and job aids on **How to Work with Transitions.**

ACTIVITY 8-2
Applying Transitions

Before You Begin
The file My Develetech Ind_Delivery.pptx is open.

Scenario
You submitted the presentation to your supervisor for final approval. She approved the content and the overall look of the presentation, but she feels the still transitions between the slides are too dull for the subject matter. She has asked you to add transitions between the slides to add more energy to the presentation.

1. Add a transition between slides.
   a) In the left pane, navigate to slide **1**.
   b) Select the **Transitions** tab and, in the **Transition to This Slide** group, select the **More** button.
   c) In the gallery, in the **Exciting** section, select **Switch**.
   d) Select **Transitions→Preview→Preview**.

2. Modify the transition.
   a) Select **Transitions→Transition to This Slide→Effect Options→Left**.
   b) In the **Timing** group, use the **Duration** field's spin buttons to change the transition duration to **02.00** seconds.
   c) Select **Transitions→Preview→Preview**.

3. Apply the transition to all slides in the presentation.
   a) Select **Transitions→Timing→Apply To All**.
   b) Select **Slide Show→Start Slide Show→From Beginning**.
   c) Navigate to various slides by using mouse-clicks or keyboard shortcuts.
   d) Press the **Esc** key to exit the slide show.
   e) Save the file.

TOPIC C

Print Your Presentation

Your presentation is now complete! At this point, you are confident that you can stand in front of the audience and deliver an effective, engaging, high-impact presentation. However, you might want to reference your speaker notes to ensure you don't skip any important information during the presentation. Additionally, you may wish to print handouts to help the audience keep track of the presentation, or to take notes.

PowerPoint 2016 gives you several options for printing hard copies of your presentation depending on your particular need. In addition to giving you the security of having your content in hand during a presentation, access to hard copies can be a lifesaver in the event of a computer crash or other technical problem.

The Print Command

The *Print command* provides you with a variety of options for printing hard copies of your presentation, both for your benefit and the benefit of the audience. The **Print** screen displays two panes—the left pane and the right pane. The left pane displays the print settings and print options, whereas the right pane displays a preview of the currently selected print options. You can use the commands in the left pane to tailor the print options to suit your needs.

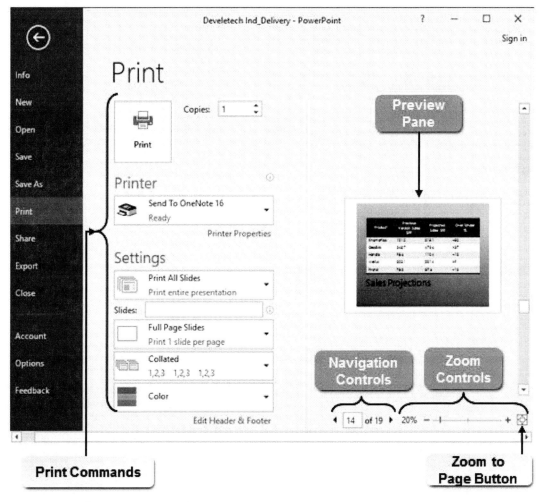

Figure 8–7: The Print command options.

The following table describes the **Print** command options.

Print Option	Allows You To
Print	Select the number of copies you wish to print, and print your presentation.
Printer drop-down menu	Select your printing destination.
Print All Slides drop-down menu	Select between printing all slides or printing only specific slides.
Slides field	Determine which slides to print if you are not printing the entire presentation.
Full Page Slides drop-down menu	Select from among printing full page slides, notes, outlines, or handouts. You can also set other printing options such as scaling the printing to fit the paper.
Print One Side drop-down menu	Switch between printing on one side of the paper or both sides.
Collated drop-down menu	Choose between collating or not collating your printouts.
Color drop-down menu	Select full-color printing, grayscale printing, or black and white printing.

> **Note: PowerPoint Online App**
>
> When you print in PowerPoint Online, the required steps vary slightly from those used to print PowerPoint 2016 files. You continue to have the ability to preview how the printout will look. However, because the settings are not readily visible on the Print tab in **Backstage** view, you will need to follow the prompts to access the print and page setup options.
>
> The first noticeable differences is when you select **FILE→Print→Print**, a PDF is created and you are prompted to preview the PDF. You can then modify the settings in the Print dialog box, as desired.

Handouts

Handouts are printed materials that the audience can use to follow along with a presentation and take notes. In addition to printing handouts by using the **Print** command, you can use PowerPoint to create a Microsoft® Word document version of your handouts. Typically, the handouts will display page numbers and the presentation date for the audience to reference.

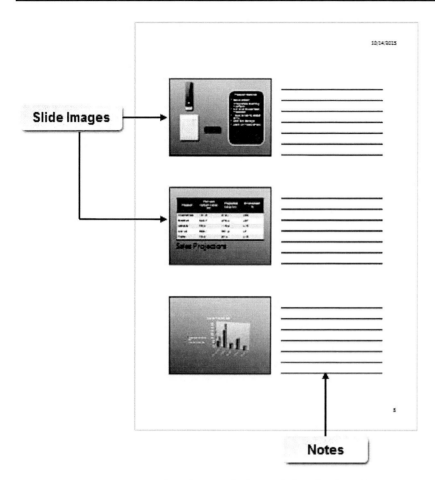

Slide Images

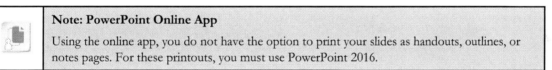

Notes

Figure 8-8: A PowerPoint handout with three slides displayed per page.

Note: PowerPoint Online App

Using the online app, you do not have the option to print your slides as handouts, outlines, or notes pages. For these printouts, you must use PowerPoint 2016.

Outlines

Outlines are printed materials that display all of the text, but none of the graphics, from the slides in a presentation. The text is displayed along with the slide numbers to help people follow along with the presentation.

1 ☐ **TRAINING NEW EMPLOYEES**
Presenter Name
Presentation Date

2 ☐ **New Employee Orientation**
· Getting to know your new assignment
· Familiarizing yourself with your new environment
· Meeting new colleagues

3 ☐ **New Work**

4 ☐ **New Environment**

5 ☐ **New Colleagues**

6 ☐ **Welcome**

7 ☐ **Today's Overview**

8 ☐ **Learning Objectives**
· Technology
· Procedure
· Policies
· Benefits

9 ☐ **NEW WORK**

10 ☐ **New Work**
The technology learning curve

11 ☐ **Who's Who**

12 ☐ **Working Toward Mastery**

13 ☐ **Doing Your Best Work**
· Working from home
· Working offsite
· Technology requirements

Figure 8–9: A presentation outline.

Notes Pages

Notes pages are printed materials that show the speaker notes, slide numbers, and the images from slides in a presentation. This printout is ideal for delivering your presentation.

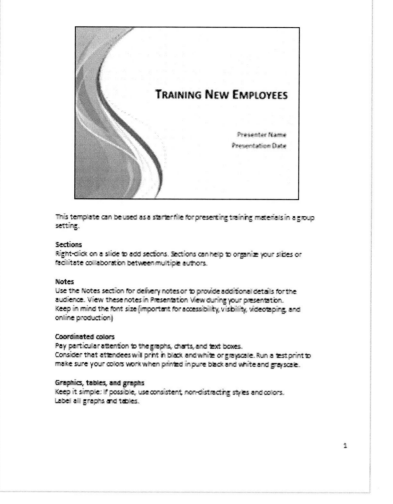

Figure 8-10: A notes page from a PowerPoint presentation.

Full Page Slides

Full page slides are printed materials that display only the slides in a presentation. Full page slides do not include speaker notes or space for the audience to take notes. On-screen text, however, is displayed as it is shown on the slides.

Figure 8-11: A full page slide from a PowerPoint presentation.

 Access the Checklist tile on your **CHOICE** Course screen for reference information and job aids on **How to Print Your Presentation.**

ACTIVITY 8-3
Print a Presentation

Before You Begin

The file My Develetech Ind_Delivery.pptx is open.

Scenario

The presentation is now complete! One of your colleagues will be delivering the first presentation. She has asked you to print one set of notes for her to use during the event. She will need notes for slides 1 through 13 only. You realize you will need to adjust the print options before printing.

1. Set your print options.

    a) Select the **File** tab.
    b) In the **Backstage** view, select the **Print** tab.
    c) In the **Settings** section, in the **Slides** text box, type *1-13*

     Note: When you type specific slide numbers or a specific range of slides in the **Slides** text box, the current selection in the drop-down menu above the **Slides** text box automatically changes to **Custom Range**.

    d) Select the **Full Page Slides** drop-down menu, and in the **Print Layout** section, select **Notes Pages**.

Settings

⬚⇥⬚	**Custom Range** Enter specific slides to print ▾
Slides:	1-13 ⓘ
▭	**Notes Pages** Print slides with notes ▾
🗅🗅	**Collated** 1,2,3 1,2,3 1,2,3 ▾
▤	Portrait Orientation ▾
▬	Color ▾

Edit Header & Footer

2. Print the presentation with the selected print options.

    a) At the bottom of the print preview, select the **Next Page** ▸ and **Previous Page** ◂ buttons to navigate through the preview.
    b) From the **Printer** drop-down list, select **Microsoft Print to PDF**.
    c) Select **Print**.

    d) In the **Save Print Output As** dialog box, navigate to the **C:\091060Data\Preparing to Deliver Your Presentation** folder.

    e) In the **File name** text box, type *My Develetech Ind_Print*

    f) Select **Save**.

TOPIC D

Deliver Your Presentation

The day is here, you are just about to deliver your presentation. You have your printed notes to reference during the event, and you have printed and passed out the audience handouts. All that is left is to deliver your presentation while displaying the slides to the audience. So, how do you do that, exactly? And, what if you want to share your ideas with people who aren't in the room?

PowerPoint 2016 contains robust functionality for customizing your slide shows and for saving your presentations in various formats. These options give you complete control over your live presentation and allow you to share your content with everyone who needs to hear the message.

Presentation Options

Typically, during a slide show the computer from which you deliver your presentation will be connected to a projector, or you will be sharing your desktop in a web-conferencing application. This allows the audience members to view your slides as you present them. There are four basic options for delivering your presentations in PowerPoint 2016: from the beginning, from the current slide, as an online presentation, or as a custom slide show.

Figure 8-12: Presentation options in the Slide Show tab.

Slide Show Option	Displays Your Slide Show
From Beginning	From the first slide in a sequential order.
From Current Slide	From the currently selected slide in a sequential order.
Present Online	As a web-based broadcast that can be viewed by anyone with an Internet connection. You will need a Windows Account to broadcast a slide show.
Custom Slide Show	In a pre-determined fashion. Custom slide shows must be set up ahead of time and will display only the selected slides.

Note: PowerPoint Online App

Instead of the **Slide Show** ribbon tab, you can use the **Slide Show** view to preview your presentation. If you want to customize the presentation options, you need to use the desktop application.

Access the Checklist tile on your CHOICE Course screen for reference information and job aids on How to Present a Slide Show.

ACTIVITY 8-4
Presenting a Slide Show

Before You Begin

The file My Develetech Ind_Delivery.pptx is open.

Scenario

Your colleague has asked you to run the slide show as she delivers the presentation. You decide to specify settings to advance the slides and start the slide show from the first slide.

1. Set timings to automatically advance the slides.

   a) If necessary, navigate to slide 1 and select the **Transitions** tab.
   b) In the **Timing** group, in the **Advance Slide** section, check the **After** check box.
   c) In the **After** field, use the spin box buttons to set the time interval for the next transition to **00:20.00** seconds.

   > **Note:** In the **Timing** group, ensure that the **On Mouse Click** check box is checked so that you can also use mouse-click and keystrokes to navigate through the slide show.

   d) In the **Timing** group, select **Apply To All**.

🔊 Sound: [No Sound] ▾	Advance Slide
🕐 Duration: 02.00 ↕	☑ On Mouse Click
🔄 Apply To All	☑ After: 00:20.00 ↕

   Timing

   e) Save the file.

2. Present a slide show.

   a) Select **Slide Show→Start Slide Show→From Beginning**.
   b) To speed up your review, click the screen, or use keyboard shortcuts to advance through the slides.
   c) Press the **Esc** key to exit the slide show.

PowerPoint Presentation File Formats

Delivering your presentation live in front of an audience isn't the only way in which you can share it. PowerPoint 2016 provides you with multiple file format options for saving your presentation. The various file formats provide you with a number of different outputs, such as templates or images, that are well-suited for various uses. You can save your presentations in various file formats from the **Backstage** view.

Export

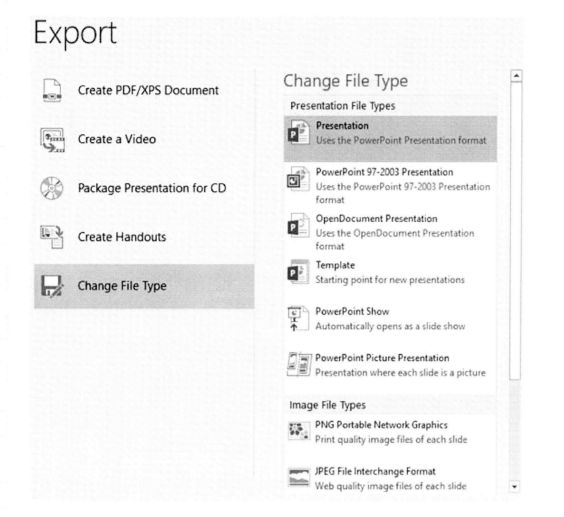

Figure 8-13: Some of the file saving options in the Backstage view.

Note: Many more file format options are available from the **Save as type** drop-down list in the **Save As** dialog box.

The following table lists some of the more commonly used file-saving options.

File Saving Option (File Extension)	Description
PowerPoint Picture Presentation (.pptx)	A PowerPoint presentation for which all slides have been converted to a picture. This reduces file size, making picture presentations ideal for storing and sharing via email. However, during the conversion process, image quality is reduced.
Portable Document Format (.pdf)/XML Paper Specification (.xps)	Saving the presentation as a .xps or a .pdf file creates a digital document that preserves formatting and makes the presentation easy to view on nearly all computers. This is ideal for sharing your presentation via email, or archiving it to a directory.
Outline (.rtf)	Saves the on-screen text from your presentation as an outline. This creates a much smaller file that is ideal for reviewing the presentation or sharing only the key points.

File Saving Option (File Extension)	Description
Open Document Presentation (.odp)	Allows you to open the presentation in presentation applications other than PowerPoint. You can also open .odp files in PowerPoint 2016.
PowerPoint Show (.ppsx)	A PowerPoint presentation that, by default, opens in the **Slide Show** view, not the **Normal** view. This is ideal for sharing the presentation with people who will also deliver it, but will not need to change the content.
Save a Slide or an Object as a Picture File (.jpg, .png)	Saves a single slide or an object as an image file.

> Access the Checklist tile on your **CHOICE Course** screen for reference information and job aids on **How to Save Your Presentation in Various File Formats**.

ACTIVITY 8-5
Exporting a Presentation to a PDF File

Before You Begin
The file My Develetech Ind_Delivery.pptx is open.

Scenario
Your colleague has asked you to email a PDF of the presentation to all of the attendees. You will first need to save the presentation as a PDF file.

---

1. Export the presentation to a PDF file.
   a) Select the **File** tab.
   b) In the **Backstage** view, select the **Export** tab.
   c) Ensure that **Create PDF/XPS Document** is selected, and then select **Create PDF/XPS**.
   d) In the **File name** text box, replace the existing text with *My Develetech Ind*
   e) In the **Save as type** drop-down list, ensure that **PDF** is selected.
   f) Select **Publish**.

2. View the published PDF file.
   a) In the **How do you want to open this file** dialog box, ensure that **Microsoft Edge** is selected and select **OK**.
   b) Scroll down to view the contents of the **My Develetech Ind.pdf** file.
   c) Close the Microsoft Edge window.

3. Close PowerPoint 2016.

Summary

In this lesson, you have successfully delivered your PowerPoint presentation. Using the various features in PowerPoint 2016 for reviewing, polishing, delivering, and sharing your presentations will give you the confidence you need to present important information whenever the need may arise. And, you now have the flexibility of knowing that you can present to an audience under a variety of circumstances and using differing technology.

What do you think is the most important aspect of preparing for a presentation?

Can you see a downside to using transitions in your presentations?

Note: Check your CHOICE Course screen for opportunities to interact with your classmates, peers, and the larger CHOICE online community about the topics covered in this course or other topics you are interested in. From the Course screen you can also access available resources for a more continuous learning experience.

Course Follow-Up

Congratulations! You have completed the *Microsoft® Office PowerPoint® 2016: Part 1 (Desktop/Office 365®)* course! You have successfully created and developed engaging multimedia presentations that use text, graphics, and animations to convey key points of your message.

The ability to communicate important information in a variety of situations will continue to be a critical skill in an increasingly connected world. In fact, it is likely to grow in importance as methods of communication become faster and more mobile. But, with the increase in the number of messages people encounter daily, comes a massive amount of clutter that can be difficult to penetrate. The effective use of engaging, dynamic, multimedia presentations is one way you can cut through the noise and make your point. With the newly acquired PowerPoint skills, you are now ready to develop effective PowerPoint presentations that deliver your message clearly and grab the audience's attention.

What's Next?

Microsoft® Office PowerPoint® 2016: Part 2 is the next course in this series. In that course, you will customize the PowerPoint environment to streamline your work flow, enhance your presentation by using more advanced graphics and animations features, collaborate on your presentation with colleagues, and utilize advanced slide show and sharing features.

Microsoft® 365®: Web Apps (with Skype® for Business) provides an introduction to using Office in a cloud-based environment. In this course, you will use Microsoft® Outlook® mail, Skype for Business instant messaging and online meetings, and Microsoft® SharePoint® Team Sites to work and collaborate on Office Online documents.

You are also encouraged to explore PowerPoint further by actively participating in any of the social media forums set up by your instructor or training administrator through the **Social Media** tile on the CHOICE Course screen.

A | Microsoft Office PowerPoint 2016 Exam 77-729

Selected Logical Operations courseware addresses Microsoft Office Specialist (MOS) certification skills for Microsoft® Office PowerPoint® 2016. The following table indicates where PowerPoint 2016 skills that are tested on Exam 77-729 are covered in the Logical Operations PowerPoint 2016 series of courses.

Objective Domain	Covered In
1. Create and Manage Presentations	
1.1 Create a Presentation	
1.1.1 Create a new presentation	Part 1, Topic 1-B
1.1.2 Create a presentation based on a template	Part 1, Topic 2-A
1.1.3 Import word document outlines	Part 1, Topic 2-A
1.2 Insert and Format Slides	
1.2.1 Insert specific slide layouts	Part 1, Topic 2-D
1.2.2 Duplicate existing slides	Part 1, Topic 2-D
1.2.3 Hide and Unhide slides	Part 1, Topic 2-D
1.2.4 Delete slides	Part 1, Topic 2-D
1.2.5 Apply a different slide layout	Part 1, Topic 2-D
1.2.6 Modify individual slide backgrounds	Part 1, Topic 2-D
1.2.7 Insert slide headers, footers, and page numbers	Part 2
1.3 Modify Slides, Handouts, and Notes	
1.3.1 Change the slide master theme or background	Part 2
1.3.2 Modify slide master content	Part 2
1.3.3 Create a slide layout	Part 2
1.3.4 Modify a slide layout	Part 2
1.3.5 Modify the handout master	Part 2
1.3.6 Modify the notes master	Part 2
1.4 Order and Group Slides	

Objective Domain	Covered In
1.4.1 Create sections	Part 2
1.4.2 Modify slide order	Part 1, Topic 2-D; Part 2
1.4.3 Rename sections	Part 2
1.5 Change Presentation Options and Views	
1.5.1 Change slide size	Part 1, Topic 2-D
1.5.2 Change views of a presentation	Part 1, Topic 2-B
1.5.3 Set file properties	Part 2
1.6 Configure a Presentation for Print	
1.6.1 Print all or part of a presentation	Part 1, Topic 8-C
1.6.2 Print notes pages	Part 1, Topic 8-C
1.6.3 Print handouts	Part 1, Topic 8-C
1.6.4 Print in color, grayscale, or black and white	Part 1, Topic 8-C
1.7 Configure and Present a Slide Show	
1.7.1 Create custom slide shows	Part 2
1.7.2 Configure slide show options	Part 2
1.7.3 Rehearse slide show timing	Part 2
1.7.4 Present a slide show by using Presenter View	Part 2
2. Insert and Format Text, Shapes, and Images	
2.1 Insert and Format Text	
2.1.1 Insert text on a slide	Part 1, Topic 2-C
2.1.2 Apply formatting and styles to text	Part 1, Topics 3-A, 3-B, 3-C
2.1.3 Apply WordArt styles to text	Part 1, Topic 3-A
2.1.4 Format text in multiple columns	Part 1, Topic 3-B
2.1.5 Create bulleted and numbered lists	Part 1, Topic 3-B
2.1.6 Insert hyperlinks	Part 2
2.2 Insert and Format Shapes and Text Boxes	
2.2.1 Insert or replace shapes	Part 1, Topic 4-B
2.2.2 Insert text boxes	Part 1, Topic 2-C
2.2.3 Resize shapes and text boxes	Part 1, Topic 5-A
2.2.4 Format shapes and text boxes	Part 1, Topic 5-B
2.2.5 Apply styles to shapes and text boxes	Part 1, Topics 4-B, 5-B
2.3 Insert and Format Images	
2.3.1 Insert images	Part 1, Topic 4-A
2.3.2 Resize and crop images	Part 1, Topic 5-A
2.3.3 Apply styles and effects	Part 1, Topic 5-B
2.4 Order and Group Objects	

Objective Domain	Covered In
2.4.1 Order objects	Part 1, Topic 2-D
2.4.2 Align objects	Part 1, Topic 5-D
2.4.3 Group objects	Part 1, Topic 5-C
2.4.4 Display alignment tools	Part 1, Topic 5-D
3. Insert Tables, Charts, SmartArt, and Media	
3.1 Insert and Format Tables	
3.1.1 Create a table	Part 1, Topic 6-A
3.1.2 Insert and delete table rows and columns	Part 1, Topic 6-B
3.1.3 Apply table styles	Part 1, Topic 6-B
3.1.4 Import a table	Part 1, Topic 6-C
3.2 Insert and Format Charts	
3.2.1 Create a chart	Part 1, Topic 7-A
3.2.2 Import a chart	Part 1, Topic 7-C
3.2.3 Change the chart type	Part 1, Topic 7-B
3.2.4 Add a legend to a chart	Part 1, Topic 7-B
3.2.5 Change the chart style of a chart	Part 1, Topic 7-B
3.3 Insert and Format SmartArt Graphics	
3.3.1 Create SmartArt Graphics	Part 2
3.3.2 Convert lists to SmartArt Graphics	Part 2
3.3.3 Add shapes to SmartArt graphics	Part 2
3.3.4 Reorder shapes in SmartArt graphics	Part 2
3.3.5 Change the color of SmartArt graphics	Part 2
3.4 Insert and Manage Media	
3.4.1 Insert audio and video clips	Part 2
3.4.2 Configure media playback options	Part 2
3.4.3 Adjust media window size	Part 2
3.4.4 Set the video start and stop time	Part 2
3.4.5 Set media timing options	Part 2
4. Apply Transitions and Animations	
4.1 Apply Slide Transitions	
4.1.1 Insert slide transitions	Part 1, Topic 8-B
4.1.2 Set transition effect options	Part 1, Topic 8-B
4.2 Animate Slide Content	
4.2.1 Apply animations to objects	Part 1, Topic 5-E
4.2.2 Apply animations to text	Part 2
4.2.3 Set animation effect options	Part 1, Topic 5-E

Objective Domain	Covered In
4.2.4 Set animation paths	Part 1, Topic 5-E
4.3 Set Timing for Transitions and Animations	
4.3.1 Set transition effect duration	Part 1, Topic 8-B
4.3.2 Configure transition start and finish options	Part 1, Topics 8-B, 8-D; Part 2
4.3.3 Reorder animations on a slide	Part 2
5. Manage Multiple Presentations	
5.1 Merge Content from Multiple Presentations	
5.1.1 Insert slides from another presentation	Part 1, Topic 2-D
5.1.2 Compare two presentations	Part 2
5.1.3 Insert comments	Part 2
5.1.4 Review comments	Part 2
5.2 Finalize Presentations	
5.2.1 Protect a presentation	Part 2
5.2.2 Inspect a presentation	Part 1, Topic 8-A; Part 2
5.2.3 Proof a presentation	Part 1, Topic 8-A
5.2.4 Preserve presentation content	Part 2
5.2.5 Export presentations to other formats	Part 1, Topic 8-C, 8-D; Part 2

B Microsoft PowerPoint 2016 Common Keyboard Shortcuts

The following table lists common keyboard shortcuts you can use in PowerPoint 2016.

Function	Shortcut
Change the font of selected text	**Ctrl+Shift+F**
Change the font size of selected text	**Ctrl+Shift+P**
Open the Find dialog box	**Ctrl+F**
Copy the selected text	**Ctrl+C**
Paste copied content	**Ctrl+V**
Select all	**Ctrl+A**
Undo the last action	**Ctrl+Z**
Apply or remove bold formatting	**Ctrl+B**
Apply or remove italic formatting	**Ctrl+I**
Apply or remove underline formatting	**Ctrl+U**
Insert a hyperlink	**Ctrl+K**
Center a paragraph	**Ctrl+E**
Justify a paragraph	**Ctrl+J**
Left align a paragraph	**Ctrl+L**
Right align a paragraph	**Ctrl+R**
Start a presentation from the beginning	**F5**
Advance to the next slide	**N** or **Enter**
Return to the previous slide	**P** or **Backspace**
Go to slide *number*	*number*+**Enter**
End a presentation	**Esc**
View the All Slides dialog box	**Ctrl+S**
Increase sound volume	**Alt+Up**
Decrease sound volume	**Alt+Down**

Mastery Builders

Mastery Builders are provided for certain lessons as additional learning resources for this course. Mastery Builders are developed for selected lessons within a course in cases when they seem most instructionally useful as well as technically feasible. In general, Mastery Builders are supplemental, optional unguided practice and may or may not be performed as part of the classroom activities. Your instructor will consider setup requirements, classroom timing, and instructional needs to determine which Mastery Builders are appropriate for you to perform, and at what point during the class. If you do not perform the Mastery Builders in class, your instructor can tell you if you can perform them independently as self-study, and if there are any special setup requirements.

Mastery Builder 2–1
Creating a Presentation

Activity Time: 5 minutes

Data File

C:\091060Data\Developing a PowerPoint Presentation\Design Team Review Process.docx

Before You Begin

Microsoft Office Word 2016 is installed.

Scenario

At an upcoming development team meeting, your team will be compiling ideas for a new design review process. You have volunteered to create a PowerPoint presentation that will be used to present the ideas to your department's director. Your team will populate the presentation with the team's best ideas. For easy comparison, you decide to include the old process highlights from an existing document.

1. Launch PowerPoint 2016, and create a new blank presentation.

2. Enter the title *Proposed Review Processes* and the subtitle *A New Way Forward*.

3. Apply the **Wisp** theme to the presentation.

4. Insert two Section Header slides as slides 2 and 3.

5. Enter the title *Old Process* and the subtitle *Highlights* on slide 2.

6. Enter the title *Proposed Process* and the subtitle *Highlights* on slide 3.

7. Insert two blank slides as slides 4 and 5.

8. Launch the **Design Team Review Process.docx** file.

9. Copy and paste the "High Level Process" text and the bulleted list from the Word document to slide 4, keeping the source formatting.

10. Close the Word document.

11. Move slide 4 so that it follows slide 2.

12. Apply a pattern fill to the background of all slides.

13. Save the file to the **C:\091060Data\Developing a PowerPoint Presentation folder** as *My Proposal.pptx*.

14. Close the file.

Mastery Builder 3-1
Editing Text

Activity Time: 10 minutes

Data File

C:\091060Data\Performing Advanced Text Editing Operations\Media 201.pptx

Scenario

You are a communications professor at a local community college. You are putting together an orientation presentation for the students on the first day of class. So far, you have only included default text on the slides in your presentation. You know this will not hold the students' interest, so you decide to apply text formatting to make the presentation look better.

---

1. Launch the **Media 201.pptx** file.

2. Apply a WordArt style to the title text on slide **1**.

3. Change the font of the subtitle text on slide **1** to **Arial Black**, change the font color to dark blue, and change the font size to **28**.

4. Apply a different WordArt style from the one you used on slide 1 to the title text on slide **2**.

5. Use the **Format Painter** tool to copy the formatting from the title text on slide **2**, and apply it to the title text on slides **3** through **6**.

6. Change the numbered list on slide **2** to a bulleted list.

7. Change the existing text on slide **5** into a bulleted list with "Groups will:" as a header, removing "Groups will" from each of the bullets in the list.

8. Add a border and a gradient fill to the text box on slide **2**.

9. Set the text box formatting from the text box on slide **2** as the default text box formatting.

10. Copy and paste the text box formatting from slide **2** to the text boxes on the remaining slides.

11. Add a text box to slide **6**, and then type *?* into the text box.

12. Center the "?" in the text box on slide **6** both horizontally and vertically.

13. Increase the font size of the "?" to **100**, and then move the text box so that it is centered below the title text.

14. Save the file to the **C:\091060Data\Performing Advanced Text Editing Operations** folder as *My Media 201.pptx* and then close the file.

Mastery Builder 4-1
Adding Images to a Presentation

Activity Time: 10 minutes

Data Files

C:\091060Data\Adding Graphical Elements to Your Presentation\Company Awards.pptx

C:\091060Data\Adding Graphical Elements to Your Presentation\Group.JPG

Scenario

Your boss is delivering an awards presentation highlighting the accomplishments of the top performing departments within the company. Although all of the text is in place, your boss feels that an image representative of each of the departments would enhance the look of the presentation. She has asked you to add appropriate images to the slides for the winning departments.

---

1. Open the **Company Awards.pptx** file.

2. On slide **4**, insert the **C:\091060Data\Adding Graphical Elements to Your Presentation\Group.JPG** image.

3. Drag the image you inserted to move it to the lower-left corner of the slide.

4. On slide **5**, insert an illustration or photograph that represents money using Bing Image Search.

5. Drag the image you inserted to move it to the lower-left corner of the slide.

6. On slide **6**, at the lower-left corner, draw a **Cloud** callout shape.

7. Apply a shape style to the cloud callout shape.

8. Save the file to the **C:\091060Data\Adding Graphical Elements to Your Presentation** folder as *My Company Awards.pptx*.

9. Close the file.

Mastery Builder 5-1
Working with Objects

Activity Time: 10 minutes

Data File

C:\091060\Modifying Objects in Your Presentation\Winter Wonder.pptx

Scenario

You and your business partner own a ski and snowboarding shop. You are pitching your advertising ideas to a marketing agency that you view as a potential vendor. The goal of the marketing campaign is to get customers thinking about winter in terms of fun, not misery. You like the images that you have selected for the presentation you will deliver, but you feel some of them could be made a bit livelier. You decide to modify some of the images to help express your vision to the marketing agency's creative director.

1. Open the **Winter Wonder.pptx** file.

2. In slide **2**, remove the background of the image of the skier.

3. Drag the image of the skier and place it in front of the winter image so that it is centered.

4. Group the two images together, and then center the group horizontally on the slide.

5. Select only the image of the skier, and then set the black color on the image transparent by using the **Set Transparent Color** option.

6. In slide **3**, apply the **Photocopy** artistic effect to the image of the skier.

7. In slide **4**, scale the image of the cabin so that it is the same height as the image of the snowboarder.

8. In slide **4**, align the image of the cabin vertically with the image of the snowboarder, and then center it horizontally below the text box with the text "People Hunker Down."

9. In slide **5**, apply an animation effect to the image so that it flies in from the top-right corner of the slide.

10. Preview the animation effect.

11. Save the file to the **C:\091060Data\Modifying Objects in Your Presentation** folder as *My Winter Wonder.pptx*.

12. Close the file.

Mastery Builder 7-1
Working with Tables and Charts

Activity Time: 20 minutes

Data Files

C:\091060Data\Adding Charts to Your Presentation\Sales Meeting.pptx

C:\091060Data\Adding Charts to Your Presentation\Sales Overview.xlsx

Scenario

You are concerned about the recent decrease in sales for your company compared to last fiscal year. You have called an emergency meeting with department heads to discuss the matter. You decide that presenting a chart that visually displays the sales drop will grab people's attention at the meeting. You have the sales figures in a Microsoft Excel worksheet, so you decide to add the worksheet to your presentation and to use the data from the worksheet to create the chart.

---

1. Open the **Sales Meeting.pptx** file.

2. In slide **4**, in the title text placeholder, type *Sales Drop*.

3. In slide **4**, create a table with five columns and three rows.

4. Open the **Sales Overview.xlsx** file in Microsoft Excel.

5. Copy the data from the Excel worksheet into the cells of the table in slide 4, and then close the **Sales Overview.xlsx** file.

6. Apply a table style to the table so that it fits well with the presentation.

7. Center the text in the table cells vertically and horizontally.

8. Increase the font size of the table text to **20**.

9. Position the table so that it is aligned appropriately below the title text both horizontally and vertically.

10. In slide **5**, create a **3-D Clustered Bar** chart.

11. Modify the chart data worksheet so that it contains two categories and four series, and then delete all data outside of the range.

12. Copy and paste the data from the table in slide 4, into the chart data worksheet. Use the destination formatting.

13. Switch the X and the Y axes for the chart, and then close the chart data worksheet.

---

14. Change the chart type to **3-D Line**.

15. Add a title to the chart.

16. Apply formatting to the **Back Wall**, the **Side Wall**, and the **Floor**.

17. Increase the chart's height to **5.0"** by scaling it up.

18. Center the chart on the slide.

19. Save the file to the **C:\091060Data\Adding Charts to Your Presentation** folder as *My Sales Meeting.pptx*.

20. Close the file.

Mastery Builder 8-1
Preparing for and Delivering a Presentation

Activity Time: 10 minutes

Data File

C:\091060Data\Preparing to Deliver Your Presentation\Winter Wonder Final.pptx

Scenario

You are ready to deliver your marketing campaign presentation to a potential vendor for your ski and snowboard shop. You decide it would be a good idea to check for errors and to print your slide notes before the meeting. You also want to liven up the presentation by adding slide transitions.

---

1. From the **C:\091060Data\Preparing to Deliver Your Presentation** folder, open the **Winter Wonder Final.pptx** file.

2. Run the Spelling Checker feature and correct the spelling errors in the presentation.

3. On slide **3**, use the thesaurus to select an alternate word for "Imagine."

4. Apply the **Shred** transition, with a duration of **1.5** seconds, to all slides in the presentation.

5. View a print preview of the slide notes.

6. Run a slide show to review the presentation.

7. Save the file to the **C:\091060Data\Preparing to Deliver Your Presentation** folder as *My Winter Wonder Final.pptx*.

8. Close PowerPoint 2016.

Glossary

Accessibility Checker
A PowerPoint feature that displays a list of the content in your presentation that may prove difficult for some people to access, displays additional information about the accessibility issues, and provides a link to Help articles on related subjects.

Animation Painter tool
A PowerPoint feature that allows users to reapply animation effects to multiple objects.

AutoCorrect feature
A PowerPoint feature that automatically corrects common spelling and capitalization errors.

Autofit feature
A PowerPoint feature that allows users to automatically fit text within text boxes and shapes regardless of the amount of text entered.

background styles
The colors and textures of slide backgrounds. These can be determined by applying themes to slides or through customization.

Backstage view
A PowerPoint user interface component that appears when users select the File tab. The Backstage view contains vertically aligned tabs that provide users with groups of related commands associated with managing files and configuring PowerPoint settings.

cells
Containers for numerical data and other content that make up a table.

character formats
Particular attributes that users can apply to the text in a presentation.

chart layouts
Pre-formatted or customizable options that determine which chart elements, such as labels, titles, and legends, will appear, and where they appear, on a chart.

chart styles
Quick Styles that users can apply to charts.

charts
Graphical representations of numerical or mathematical data.

clipboard
A task pane that allows users to paste copied text and graphical elements within Microsoft Office applications.

Compatibility Checker
A PowerPoint feature that displays a list of possible compatibility issues in your presentation and provides links to Help material to resolve them.

contextual tabs
Highly specialized tabs that appear on the ribbon when certain objects are selected. These contain specific commands and menus related to items such as tables, charts, and pictures.

cropping

Removing particular regions of an image to display only the desired image elements.

dialog box launchers

Small buttons with downward-facing arrows on the bottom-right corner of some ribbon functional groups. These buttons open dialog boxes that contain additional commands specific to the functional groups.

embedding

The process of placing a copy of an object from a source file into a presentation. Changes in the source file are not reflected in the presentation.

Eyedropper tool

A tool which displays within several PowerPoint 2016 menus and allows users to apply color to objects based on the color of another on-slide element.

Format Painter

A PowerPoint tool that allows users to copy object or text formatting, and then apply the formatting to other objects or text.

full page slides

Printed materials that display only the slides in a presentation.

galleries

Rectangular menus that display a variety of related visual options for objects in a presentation.

gridlines

Multiple horizontal and vertical dotted lines that form a grid, which allows users to accurately position objects on a slide.

Grouping feature

PowerPoint feature that allows users to link multiple objects together, effectively making them a single object.

guides

Lines that allow users to accurately position objects on a slide. By default, these lines divide slides into four equal sections and intersect at the exact center of the slides.

handouts

Printed materials that the audience can use to follow along with a presentation and take notes.

image compression

The process of reducing the file size of an image.

Insights

A new feature in PowerPoint 2016 that uses the Bing search tool to perform a smart lookup operation on the Internet.

KeyTip

Descriptive text that displays the keyboard shortcut for a command.

linking

The process of importing an object into a presentation in which the data is stored in the source file. When the source file is changed, the changes are reflected in the imported object.

Live Preview feature

PowerPoint feature that displays a temporary preview of formatting changes. This feature allows users to view various formatting options before they are selected.

Mini toolbar

A floating toolbar that appears next to selected objects on slides and provides users with access to some of the most commonly used commands without having to navigate the ribbon.

notes pages

Printed materials that display the speaker notes, slide numbers, and the images from the slides in a presentation.

Notes pane

A PowerPoint user interface component that allows users to enter notes that can be referenced during the delivery of a presentation.

object order
A function of PowerPoint that defines how objects that overlap on slides appear in relation to each other. The state of being located in front of or behind other objects.

Open screen
PowerPoint 2016 screen that allows users to select and launch a previously saved presentation for editing.

orientation
The angle at which an object displays on a slide.

outlines
Printed materials that display all of the text, but none of the graphics, from the slides in a presentation.

Paste Preview
A PowerPoint feature that displays a temporary preview of paste commands. This feature allows users to view various pasting options before they are selected.

Paste Special command
A PowerPoint feature that allows users to paste objects to a new location as a specific type of file.

Photo Album feature
A PowerPoint feature that allows users to insert and display photographs in a custom presentation.

Print command
Provides users with a variety of options for printing hard copies of a presentation.

Quick Access Toolbar
A PowerPoint user interface component that provides users with easy access to commonly used commands.

quick layouts
Pre-formatted layouts that users can apply to charts in PowerPoint 2016.

Quick Styles
Themes that can be quickly applied to a particular object by selecting a single command button.

Remove Background tool
PowerPoint tool that allows users to remove the background from images, leaving only the desired subject elements in the image.

Replace Font option
A PowerPoint feature that allows users to replace all text of a particular font type to another font type throughout a presentation.

resizing
The process of changing the height and width of an object without necessarily maintaining the ratio of height to width.

ribbon
A PowerPoint user interface component that contains task-specific command buttons and menus grouped together under sets of tabs and functional groups.

rotation handle
Component of object borders, which appear when the object is selected, that allows users to rotate objects on slides.

rulers
Visual reference tools used to accurately position objects on slides.

Save As screen
PowerPoint 2016 screen that provides users with the ability to name and select a destination for presentation files.

scaling
The process of changing the height and width of an object while maintaining the ratio of height to width.

ScreenTip
Descriptive text that appears when you hover the cursor over a command or a button. The text displays the command name or style option, and may include a brief description of the command.

shapes
Common geometric objects that users can add to presentations.

sizing handles
Component of object borders, which appear when the object is selected, that allow users to increase or decrease the size of objects on slides.

slide layouts
Templates that determine the placement of various content types on slides.

slides
Individual presentation objects that are used to display content to the audience.

slideshow
A presentational feature of PowerPoint that displays slides on screen in a particular sequence.

spacing
The vertical distance between lines of text or paragraphs.

Spelling Checker feature
A PowerPoint feature that scans all of the text in a presentation to check for spelling errors.

Start screen
First screen that displays when a user launches PowerPoint 2016. From here, users can create a new file, access previously saved files, and access templates and themes.

status bar
A PowerPoint user interface component that appears along the bottom of the PowerPoint window. The status bar contains information about the currently selected slide and provides the user with access to commands for some of the basic viewing features within PowerPoint.

Switch Row/Column feature
A PowerPoint feature that allows users to change the orientation of data along the X and Y axes of a chart without having to re-enter the data.

tables
Containers for numerical data and other content that are organized into columns and rows of individual cells.

Tell Me
A new feature in PowerPoint 2016 that enables you to quickly find specific functions within the PowerPoint interface.

template
An existing presentation that contains content placeholders that are already formatted.

text boxes
Blank containers for adding text to slides in PowerPoint.

text placeholders
Containers for instructional text indicating the type of content users should enter.

theme variants
Collections of closely related themes that share many of the same layout and design elements, but with some changes.

themes
Combinations of colors, fonts, and effects that provide a consistent look and feel throughout a presentation.

thesaurus
Research tool that provides users with a list of synonyms and antonyms for a particular word.

Thumbnails pane
A PowerPoint user interface component that, by default, appears on the left side of the screen and allows users to access and navigate the slides in a presentation.

transitions
Visual effects that occur as users advance from one slide to the next in a slide show.

WordArt styles
Predetermined formatting configurations that can be applied to the text in a presentation.

Index

V

view options, color *16*
View tab *15*

W

WordArt styles *71*